The Ivory Tower

The Ivory Tower

Essays in Philosophy and Public Policy

ANTHONY KENNY

Basil Blackwell

© Anthony Kenny 1985

First published 1985

Basil Blackwell Ltd
108 Cowley Road, Oxford OX4 1JF, UK

Basil Blackwell Inc.
432 Park Avenue South, Suite 1505,
New York, NY 10016, USA

British Library Cataloguing in Publication Data
Kenny, Anthony
The ivory tower: essays in philosophy and public policy.
1. Philosophy
I. Title
192   B1646.K4

ISBN 0-631-13985-0

Library of Congress Cataloging in Publication Data
Kenny, Anthony John Patrick.
The ivory tower.

Includes index.
Contents: pt. 1. Philosophy and law –
Direct and oblique intention and malice aforethought –
Intention and mens rea in murder – [etc.]
1. Law–Philosophy–Addresses, essays, lectures.
2. Criminal intent–Addresses, essays, lectures.
3. Nuclear warfare–Addresses, essays, lectures.
4. Academic freedom–Addresses, essays, lectures.
I. Title
K235.K43 1985   340'.112   85–3884
ISBN 0-631-13985-0

Typeset by Katerprint Co. Ltd, Oxford
Printed in Great Britain by
The Bath Press Ltd, Avon

Contents

Introduction

Philosophers are sometimes accused of living in an ivory tower, remote from the practical concerns of real life. This is a distortion of the truth. There may be areas of philosophy, as there are areas of mathematics, which are unrelated to business or politics and which are of little interest to the non-specialist. But some of the cardinal philosophical problems connect closely with issues of universal concern, and the conceptual clarity that the philosopher seeks is precious to the decision-maker no less than to the theoretician.

My own philosophical studies have been concerned especially with the philosophy of mind, or philosophical psychology. The philosopher of mind investigates the concepts which we use in describing and understanding mental states, processes and activities, and the framework by which we make intelligible human action and conduct. The ideas which he studies and strives to make luminous are those which are the fundamental prerequisites of moral, legal and political thinking. Philosophy of this kind does not stand at a distance from practical life: human activity is its very subject matter.

The philosophical essays in this book are concerned, literally, with matters of life and death. They deal with the way in which murder is to be defined, and with the types of plea which may be made in mitigation or exculpation of the taking of life. They are concerned with the logic and ethics of nuclear warfare and nuclear deterrence, and the way in which traditional moral principles can be applied to the conditions of the twentieth century.

Though the essays deal with vital legal and political issues, they are not intended simply as a philosopher's reflections on these issues. They are themselves essays in philosophy. For through the different topics treated there runs a single thread of philosophical concern: the analysis of mental states such as intention, voluntariness, purpose. For the debate among lawyers on the definition of murder is enmeshed in philosophical problems about the concept of intention; and the morality of different kinds of intention plays an important role also in the arguments about the legitimacy of nuclear deterrence.

The first part of the book contains essays on the area where philosophy of mind overlaps with law. The first, 'Direct and Oblique Intention and Malice Aforethought' was published in the *Kingston Law Review* in spring 1976; the second, 'Intention and *Mens Rea* in Murder', appeared in the Festschrift for H.L.A. Hart entitled *Law, Morality and Society*, edited by P. Hacker and J. Raz (Oxford University Press, 1977). These essays discuss the definition of murder implicit in the historic decision of the House of Lords in the case of *Hyam* in 1974. As an appended note explains, the decision in that case still defines the legal boundaries of the concept today. The third essay, 'Duress *per Minas* as a Defence to Crime' was a reply to a contribution on the same topic by Lord Kilbrandon at a Royal Institute of Philosophy conference on the philosophy of law in September 1979. The final essay of the first part, 'The Expert in Court' (The Blackstone Lecture of 1982), concerns the general topic of expert evidence, but it has particular reference to the use of psychiatric evidence when a defence of insanity or diminished responsibility is led in homicide cases.

The second part of the book is concerned with the morality of the use and possession of nuclear weapons. The first essay here is the oldest one of the collection. It first appeared in *The Clergy Review* in December 1962, and was subsequently reprinted in a collection edited by Walter Stein entitled *Nuclear Weapons and Christian Conscience* (The Merlin Press, 1963, 1981). It was written from a Catholic viewpoint and contains some Catholic assumptions which I no longer share; but I have reprinted it because it is continuous with the more recent essays which make up the body of this section, and because after 20 years the main issues of both the religious and strategic debate about nuclear weapons have altered remarkably little. The next essay, 'Better Dead than Red' appeared in a collection of papers by philosophers edited by Nigel Blake and Kay Pole under the title *Objections to Nuclear Defence* (Routledge and

Kegan Paul, 1984). The last two papers in this section, which form a unity, have not been published but were delivered to a seminar in Oxford in Hilary Term 1984.

The final paper is the most recent contribution I have made to the area where philosophy and polity overlap: a lecture on academic freedom delivered on a visit to the University of Cape Town in July 1984. It provides an epilogue to a volume designed to illustrate that the free debate of philosophical ideas is of value not only within the academy but also in the wider world.

Part I

Philosophy and Law

1

Direct and Oblique Intention and Malice Aforethought
(1976)

Jeremy Bentham, followed by other philosophers, made a distinction between direct and oblique intention. Something was directly intentional if it was something sought as an end in itself or as a means to an end; something was obliquely intentional if it was neither an end nor a means but merely a foreseen consequence of one's directly intentional actions. The distinction has numerous everyday applications: if I get up in the middle of the night to get a drink of water, knowing it's likely that I'll wake the baby but hoping very much that I won't, then getting a drink and getting out of bed are directly intentional, while waking the baby (if the brat wakes after all) is only obliquely intentional.

Since (at least) *Vickers* [1957] 2 QB 644 it has been accepted that 'the intention either to kill or to do some grievous bodily harm' constitutes malice aforethought in the crime of murder. Since (at least) *Desmond* [1868] it has been accepted that the intention required for murder was merely oblique, not necessarily direct, intention: authorities have differed over the degree of certainty required in the foresight constituting the oblique intention. The decision of the House of Lords in *Smith* [1961] AC 290 was widely taken to mean that not even oblique intention was necessary: if a reasonable man would have foreseen grievous bodily harm as the consequence of a certain course of action by the accused, the accused could be guilty of murder without even obliquely intending either death or grievous bodily harm. To meet the widespread discontent with the state of the law after *Smith* the Law Commission in 1967[1] proposed two reforms. It suggested that no court or jury should be bound to infer that a man intended or foresaw the

[1] Law Commission No. 10 Imputed Criminal Intent *(DPP* v. *Smith)*.

natural and probable consequence of his actions. It also recommended that killing shall not amount to murder unless done with intent to kill; a man has such an intent 'if he means his actions to kill, or if he is willing for his actions, though meant for another purpose, to kill in accomplishing that purpose'.

The first but not the second of these recommendations was embodied in the Criminal Justice Act of 1967. If the second recommendation had been accepted, death which was obliquely intentional would still count as murder: for if one fails to desist from a course of action one knows is likely to cause death, then one is willing for one's actions to kill in accomplishing one's purposes: this is a minimum form of willingness which we might call 'mere consent'.

The acceptance by the Criminal Justice Act of 1967 of only one half of the recommendation by which the Law Commission hoped to undo the undesirable effects of the *Smith* decision left the definition of murder in a confused state which a 1974 case gave the House of Lords an opportunity to clarify. (*R.* v. *Hyam*, HL(E), [1974] 2 WLR 607.) The accused in this case was a woman who had had a relationship with a man who became engaged to be married to *B*. In the early hours of the morning she went to *B*'s house and poured petrol through the letter box, stuffed newspaper through and lit it. She gave *B* no warning but went home leaving the house burning. *B* escaped from the house but her two daughters were suffocated by the fumes of the fire and the accused was charged with their murder. Her defence was that she had set fire to the house only in order to frighten *B* so that she whould leave the neighbourhood. The jury were directed by the trial judge to concentrate on the intent to do serious bodily harm, and told that the prosecution had proved the necessary intent if the jury were satisfied that when she had set fire to the house she had known it was highly probable that the fire would cause such harm. The jury convicted, and the accused's appeal against conviction was dismissed by the Court of Appeal.

By a majority of three to two, the House of Lords dismissed the appeal. It is widely held to have ruled that a person who, without intending to endanger life, did an act knowing that it was probable that serious bodily harm would result was guilty of murder if death resulted. But the exact force of the ruling is not easy to determine.

Though the three judges of the majority agreed in dismissing the appeal, the reasons they gave appealed to three different theories of the malice aforethought required for murder, and it is of more than merely philosophical interest to follow their arguments.

Lord Hailsham began by maintaining that no degree of foresight or knowledge was enough to constitute the *mens rea* for murder. The question to be settled was whether an intention short of the intention to kill was sufficient. The Homicide Act of 1957, he maintained, had recognized as a form of malice aforethought a state called 'implied malice' which was rightly taken in *Vickers* to be the intention to do some grievous bodily harm. Parliament in 1967 in enacting the first and failing to enact the second of the two draft clauses of the Law Commission had shown that while rejecting an objective criterion for intent, it wished to retain the intention to cause grievous bodily harm as a possible alternative to intent to kill as the essential mental element in the crime of murder. It was undesirable to overrule *Smith* at this point, because there were two points in the *Smith* ruling of permanent value: (a) the definition of 'grievous bodily harm' as bodily harm which, while more serious than more interference with comfort, was not necessarily so serious as to endanger life; (b) the ruling that the unlawful and voluntary act must be aimed at someone (in order to eliminate cases of negligence or dangerous driving). The present case, in any event, did not turn on the contrast between objective and subjective criteria for intent, but rather on whether foresight is an alternative species of malice aforethought and, if so, whether a high degree of probability of what is foreseen is enough.

Lord Hailsham distinguished between two senses of motive: (a) emotion prompting an act, in the present case the appellant's jealousy of *B*, (b) purpose, end or object. Neither of these, he said, was identical with 'intention' for this 'embraces, in addition to the end, all the necessary consequences of an action including the means to the end and any consequences intended along with the end'. (p. 617). This definition, it can be seen, is close to Bentham's notion of direct intention.[2] Lord Hailsham quoted favourably an

---

[2] Though, with respect, there is the possibility of confusion in talking of means as consequences and a certain circularity in singling out *intended* consequences, and an obscurity in the nature of the 'consequences intended along with the end' unless there are further independent ends – other birds, so to speak to be killed with the same stone.

account of an earlier judge according to which 'intention' connotes a state of affairs in which the party intending 'decides, so far as in him lies, to bring about, and which in point of possibility, he has a reasonable prospect of being able to bring about, by his own act of volition'[3]. But at this point it becomes unclear whether Lord Hailsham regards direct intent so necessary: the definition, he says is a good definition 'so long as it is held to include the means as well as the end and the inseparable consequences of the end as well as the means'. Thus defined, he claims, intention is clearly distinguished from desire and foresight of probable consequences. It need not, however, be distinguished from certain consequences: taking up an example from the Law Commission, Lord Hailsham went some way in the direction of oblique intention:

> A man may desire to blow up an aircraft in flight in order to obtain insurance moneys. But if any passengers are killed he is guilty of murder, as their death will be a moral certainty if he carries out his intention. There is no difference between blowing up the aircraft and intending the death of some or all of the passengers. (p.617)

Lord Hailsham drew from the case he has so far presented the reasonable conclusion that the question 'does a knowledge that it is highly probable that one's act will result in death or serious bodily harm suffice for malice aforethought' must be answered in the negative. In the case in point, moreover, as he said the most that could be said is that 'what was intended was to expose the inhabitants of the house to the serious risk of death or grievous bodily harm' and not actually to cause death or grievous bodily harm (p. 618). He did not agree that *Desmond* showed conclusively that foresight, while not constituting intent, was an alternative species of malice aforethought. Nonetheless, he went on to qualify, indeed almost to reverse, the negative answer to the question of public importance on which the case turned. He argued as follows:

> What are we to say of the state of mind of a defendant who knows that a proposed course of conduct exposes a third party to a serious risk of death or grievous bodily harm, *without actually intending those*

[3] *Per* Asquith LJ in *Cunnliffe* v. *Goodman* [1950] 2 KB 237, 253.

consequences but nevertheless and without lawful excuse deliberately pursues that course of conduct regardless whether the consequences to his potential victim take place or not? In that case, if my analysis be correct, there is not merely actual foresight of the probable consequences *but actual intention to expose his victim to the risk* of those consequences whether they in fact occur or not. (p. 620, italics mine)

This distinction between the intention *to bring it about that p* and the intention *to bring about the risk that p* seems to me to be an important one which brings a great deal of light into this difficult area. The two intentions, Lord Hailsham says, though factually and logically distinct, are morally indistinguishable; both therefore should be treated alike, and wherever the intention *to bring it about that p* is sufficient for murder if death results the intention *to bring about the risk that p* should also be sufficient.

This seems to me a very reasonable proposal: unfortunately, Lord Hailsham does not make it clear whether he is applying the same careful distinction between foresight and intention in the case of the intention to bring about a risk as he does in the case of the intention to bring about death or grievous bodily harm. He seems to use the following formulae as equivalent descriptions of the state of mind which he wishes to characterize as malice aforethought:

a defendant who knows the risk, and deliberately pursues his course of conduct regardless . . . a man, in full knowledge of the danger involved, and without lawful excuse, deliberately does that which exposes a victim to the risk. (p. 621)

In his final summing up he says that murder must be an act committed with one or other of three intentions, of which the third is

Where the defendant knows that there is serious risk that death or grievous bodily harm will ensue from his acts, and commits those acts deliberately and without lawful excuse, the intention to expose a potential victim to that risk as the result of those acts. (p. 622)

It is not clear here whether the intention is meant to be an extra factor supervening on the knowledge, deliberation, and lack of justification of the acts, or whether the presence of those three elements is itself taken to *constitute* the third species of intention.[4]

One thing that is quite clear in Lord Hailsham's judgment is that he regards the intent to bring about a risk of grievous bodily harm as amounting to malice aforethought no less than the intent to bring about a risk of death; and no doubt in practice it would often be difficult to distinguish the two. Lord Diplock, however, thought that *Vickers* and *Smith* were wrong in allowing the intent to do grievous bodily harm as an alternative: they should have accepted the submission that in order to amount to the crime of murder the offender, if he did not intend to kill, must have intended or foreseen as a likely consequence of his act that human life would be endangered. The decisions in those cases, he argued learnedly, were based on a misreading of the history of the doctrine of constructive malice, from Lord Ellenborough's Act of 1803 which made it a felony to wound people with intent to do them grievous bodily harm, right up to the Homicide Act of 1957 which abolished the doctrine of constructive malice which had made it murder to kill in furtherance of a felony. The House of Lords should now overrule *Vickers* and *Smith* and take the opportunity, which had been lost in those cases, to restrict the relevant intention on a charge of murder to an intention to kill or to cause a bodily injury known to be likely to endanger life. The appeal should therefore be allowed. In this conclusion he was followed by Lord Kilbrandon.

On the nature of the state of mind denoted by 'intent', Lord Diplock said:

> No distinction is to be drawn in English law between the state of mind of one who does an act because he desires it to produce a particular evil consequence, and the state of mind of one who does the act knowing full well that it is likely to produce that consequence although it may not be the object he was seeking to achieve by doing this act. What is common to both these states of mind is willingness to produce the particular evil consequence: and this, in my view, is the *mens rea* needed. (p. 629)

[4] Perhaps the extra is the step from 'danger is probable' to 'the risk of danger is certain'. Since Lord Hailsham thinks that foresight of the certainty *that p* is tantamount to *intending that p*, this will explain why he thinks that foreseeing the probability of danger comes to the same as intending the risk.

This 'willingness' is what we earlier called 'consent' and have already met in the course of considering Lord Hailsham's argument.

The two judges who supported the Lord Chancellor in rejecting the appeal both refused to follow his view of the nature of the state of mind constituting *mens rea* for murder. Lord Dilhorne cited the authorities for equating intent with foresight, and those for regarding foresight as an alternative form of malice aforethought, and sided with those who equated foresight with intent.

A man may do an act with a number of intentions. If he does it deliberately and intentionally, knowing when he does it that it is highly probable that grievous bodily harm will result, I think most people would say and be justified in saying that whatever other intentions he may have had as well, he at least intended grievous bodily harm. (p. 625)

Lord Cross of Chelsea distinguished between an ordinary man's notion of intention, according to which no more than some degree of foresight was necessary – surely an IRA car bomber intends to injure those who are hurt when his bomb explodes! – and a logician's sense of intention which could not be equated with foresight; both the broad and the narower sense were sufficient to constititute malice aforethought.

Neither Lord Dilhorne nor Lord Cross was prepared without further argument to follow Lord Diplock in excluding grievous bodily harm as a possible alternative content to a murderous intent, and accordingly they dismissed the appeal.

It will be seen that of all the judges expressing an opinion on the nature of intention and its relationship to the malice aforethought required for murder, no two appear to have precisely the same concept of intention, and Lord Hailsham's speech is capable of being read as defending, in two different parts, two different and incompatible views of that concept. The positions range from the pure Benthamite view of Lord Dilhorne to the view defended in the earlier part of Lord Hailsham's speech equating intention with choice of means and ends.

To the layman it seems a pity that the House of Lords did not combine the insights of both Lord Hailsham and Lord Diplock and define the *mens rea* required for murder as being the direct intention to kill or to create a serious risk of death. If, as Lords Diplock and Kilbrandon believed, and as Lord Cross of Chelsea professed himself willing to believe, it was open to the court to reverse *Vickers* and *Smith*, then in restricting the content of murderous intent to killing and endangering life the House would have made the law of murder take the form which, in the opinion of all of them, and of all who have tried to codify the English law of homicide, it *ought* to take. And in restricting the nature of the *mens rea* to direct intention instead of allowing it to embrace foresight they would have brought greater conceptual clarity into the law and brought legal terminology more closely to common parlance.

In the particular case of *Hyam* it is perhaps not easy to settle whether she was intentionally creating a risk to life or only intentionally creating a risk of serious bodily harm. But it does not seem to be an objection to the definition suggested that it makes this case into a borderline one: it looks as if the majority of the House thought that it *ought not* to come within the definition of murder, though a majority of them thought it did so.

The difficult cases – actual and imaginary – which preoccupied their Lordships could all, it seems to me, be taken care of by the following simple definition of murder. Murder should be defined as the performance of an act which causes death with the intent either to kill or to create a serious risk of death: the intent in each case to be direct. The intent to kill should be taken to include the (direct) intent to bring about a state of affairs from which one knows death will certainly follow.

This definition will enable us to decide all the difficult cases in the way which – to me as to Lord Hailsham – intuitively seems correct. The surgeon in a risky operation will lack malice aforethought, if his patient dies, because he had no direct intent to kill or endanger him; there will be no need to invoke the sinister concept of 'lawful excuse'. The man who blows up the plane for insurance money will be guilty of murder when the passengers are killed, because though he did not directly intend to kill or endanger life, he directly intended to bring about a state of affairs of which he knew death was the certain consequence.

The other cases which presented difficulty, namely terrorist bombings, would commonly not be difficult to bring under the definition proposed: the paradigm case of terrorist bombing is where the bombing is in order to spread terror precisely by creating widespread risk to life and limb. Where the creation of risk to life is not part of the plan, and therefore not directly intended – as may be shown, for instance, by the placing of the bomb in a particular case, or by the nature of the precautions taken – then surely death which may result *should not* be taken as murder.

2

Intention and *Mens Rea* in Murder
(1977)

In a characteristically energetic and wide-ranging paper of 1967[1] H. L. A. Hart discussed *inter alia* the role of intentionality in the definition of murder. It is commonly held that English law does not require that a killing, in order to amount to murder, should be something intended in the sense that the accused set out to achieve it, either as a means or an end. Here, as Hart pointed out, the law diverges from what is ordinarily meant by expressions like 'he intentionally killed those men'.

> Some legal theorists, Bentham among them, have recorded this divergence by distinguishing (as *'oblique* intention'), mere foresight of consequences from *'direct* intention' where the consequences must have been contemplated by the accused not merely as a foreseen outcome but as an end which he set out to achieve, or as a means to an end, and constituted at least part of his reason for doing what he did. (pp. 120–1)

Hart counted it a merit of the English law of homicide that – unlike the principle of 'double effect' favoured by Catholic moral theologians – it did not pay attention to the difference between direct and oblique intention, either being sufficient to constitute murder. Both the direct and oblique cases, he argued, share a feature which any system of assigning responsibility for conduct must treat as crucial. In each type of case the situation is that the accused.

> had control over the alternative between the victims' dying or living, his choice tipped the balance; in both cases he had control over and

[1] 'Intention and Punishment', *Oxford Review*, no. 4, February 1967; reprinted in H.L.A. Hart, *Punishment and Responsibility* (Oxford University Press, 1968) pp. 113-35, to which references are given.

may be considered to have chosen the outcome, since he consciously opted for the course leading to the victims' deaths. Whether he sought to achieve this as an end or a means to his end, or merely foresaw it as an unwelcome consequence of his intervention, is irrelevant at this stage of conviction where the question of control is crucial. (p. 122)

Hart conceded, with some hesitation, that the distinction between direct and oblique intention might be relevant when determining the severity of punishment.

I have argued elsewhere[2] that even on a utilitarian theory of punishment there may be reason for distinguishing in the law of homicide between direct and oblique intention even at the stage of conviction. I shall briefly return to the moral question later in the present paper. But the main question I wish to raise is not about the justification of the current law of homicide, but about its exact content. Assuming that Hart's paper gave an accurate account of the English law of homicide in 1967, does it remain exact as an account of the law today, after the 1974 decision of the House of Lords in *Hyam* v. *DPP*?

In presenting the state of the law, Hart relied on the 1868 case *R.* v. *Desmond, Barrett and Others*. Barrett dynamited a prison wall in order to liberate two Fenians; the plot failed, but the explosion killed some persons living near by. It was clearly no part of Barrett's purpose, either as a means or an end, to kill or injure anyone, but he was convicted on the ground that he foresaw their death or serious injury. As the then Lord Chief Justice summed up, it is murder 'if a man did [an] act not with the purpose of taking life but with the knowledge or belief that life was likely to be sacrificed by it' (pp. 119–20).

In *Hyam's* case, Lord Hailsham of St Marylebone, then Lord Chancellor, questioned whether any inference to the current state of the law could be drawn from *Desmond*. The words cited above, he pointed out, came after a passage in which the doctrine of constructive malice ('felony murder') had been expounded.

---

[2] 'Intention and Purpose in Law', in *Essays in Legal Philosophy*, edited by R. S. Summers, (Oxford University Press, 1968) pp. 146–63, esp. pp. 158–60. The arguments presented there were a modified version of those in an earlier paper [*Journal of Philosophy*, 63 (1966)] searchingly criticized by Hart.

Like other 19th century cases, the direction given was at a time
when no jury could have the prisoner's sworn testimony to consider,
and when there was no adequate system of criminal appeal.
Moreover, it is not really satisfactory to charge a jury on two parallel
legal theories each leading to the same result and leave them with no
means of saying which of the two their verdict is intended to follow.
The jury itself may well have founded their verdict in *R. v. Desmond*
entirely on the doctrine of constructive malice to which, at the time,
the defence had, it would seem, no possible answer. ([1974] 2 All ER
53)

From several remarks in his speech it appeared that Lord
Hailsham believed that since the abolition of constructive malice
by the Homicide Act of 1957 a *direct* intention of some kind (to kill,
say, or to cause grievous bodily harm) was necessary to constitute
malice aforethought in murder. Thus he said 'I do not believe that
knowledge or any degree of foresight is enough' (p. 43). '"Intention" is clearly to be distinguished alike from "desire" and from
foresight of the probable consequence' (p. 52). 'I do not consider
. . . that the fact that a state of affairs is correctly foreseen as a
highly probable consequence of what is done is the same thing as
the fact that the state of affairs is intended' (p. 52). Nor is it the case
that foresight, if not identical with intent, is an alternative form of
malice aforethought. 'I do not think that foresight as such of a high
degree of probability is at all the same thing as intention, and, in
my view, it is not foresight but intention which constitutes the
mental element in murder' (p. 54). The innovation in Lord
Hailsham's speech was the proposal that the list of intentions
sufficient to constitute murder should include not only the intent to
kill and the intent to cause grievous bodily harm, but also the intent
to expose a potential victim to the serious risk of death or grievous
bodily harm.

Lord Hailsham's speech, therefore, is of interest in the present
context as setting out a view of intent in murder which is in direct
opposition to that presented and defended by Professor Hart. But
its interest is, of course, very much wider than an academic one.
Because of the circumstances of its delivery in *Hyam's* case it can be
argued that it effected a significant change in law.

The verdict in *Hyam* was given by a majority of three to two. The

other majority judges both acepted that oblique intention to kill or
to cause grievous bodily harm was sufficient for malice aforethought in murder. Lord Dilhorne said:

> Whether or not it be that the doing of the act with the knowledge
> that certain consequences are highly probable is to be treated as
> establishing the intent to bring about those consequences, I think it
> is clear that for at least 100 years such knowledge has been
> recognised as amounting to malice aforethought. (p. 59)

It was therefore not necessary to decide whether such knowledge
amounted to intent; but Lord Dilhorne was inclined to think that it
did. Lord Cross of Chelsea conceded that in a strict sense of
intention foresight of consequences that are less than certain does
not constitute intention. But foresight of death or grievous bodily
harm was none the less sufficient for malice aforethought:

> The first question to be answered is whether if an intention to kill –
> using intention in the strict sense of the word – is murder – as it
> plainly is – doing an unlawful act with knowledge that it may well
> cause death ought also to be murder. I have no doubt whatever that
> it ought to be. On this point I agree entirely with the view expressed
> by Cockburn C.J. in the passage in his summing up in *R. v. Desmond*
> . . . I think that it is right that the doing of an act which one realises
> may well cause grievous bodily harm should also constitute malice
> aforethought whether or not one realises that one's act may
> endanger life. (p. 71)

In *Hyam* therefore we have a situation parallel to the unsatisfactory one to which Lord Hailsham drew attention in *Desmond:* the
appeal was dismissed on the basis of three different parallel theories
of intent and malice aforethought. But of the three theories the one
which is crucial to study with a view to seeing the effect which the
ratio decidendi of *Hyam* will have on the future history of the English
law of homicide is that of Lord Hailsham. For, as I hope to show, it
is that theory which draws the definition of murder in the
narrowest manner: and though the actions of the appellant Hyam
fell within the definition of murder on all three theories, it is not
hard to think of cases which would be murder according to the

accounts of Lords Dilhorne and Cross, but not according to Lord Hailsham's proposal.

Lord Hailsham did not in presenting his opinion make use of Bentham's distinction between direct and oblique intention, but at least in the first part of his speech it is obvious that it is direct intention that he has in mind. He distinguished between intention on the one hand and motive (in the sense of 'emotion prompting an act') and purpose (in the sense of 'ultimate end of a course of action') on the other (pp. 51–2). Direct intention which is the intending something as a means *or* as an end, is likewise to be distinguished from motive and purpose in the senses in question. Lord Hailsham went on: 'Intention . . . embraces, in addition to the end, all the necessary consequences of an action including the means to the end and any consequences intended along with the end' (p. 52). This makes clear that intention for Hailsham, like direct intention for Bentham, includes means as well as ends. To clarify his position further Lord Hailsham quoted with approval the definition of 'intention' given by an earlier judge in a civil case:

> An 'intention' to my mind connotes a state of affairs which the party 'intending' – I will call him X – does more than merely contemplate: it connotes a state of affairs which, on the contrary, he decides, so far as in him lies, to bring about and which, in point of possibility, he has a reasonable prospect of being able to bring about, by his own act of volition.

This definition, which clearly would exclude merely oblique intention, is said by Lord Hailsham to be a good definition for purposes of criminal law 'so long as it is held to include the means as well as the end and the inseparable consequences of the end as well as the means'. By 'inseparable consequences' he means those which follow with moral certainty from the achievement of the end. He cites an imaginary case from the Law Commission's disquisition on Imputed Intent: 'a man may desire to blow up an aircraft in flight in order to obtain insurance moneys. But if any passengers are killed he is guilty of murder, as their death will be a moral certainty if he carries out his intention' (p. 52).

Bentham, when he distinguished direct from oblique intention, did not consider the case of inseparable consequences. One might argue that these should count as merely obliquely intended, since foresight even with certainty, remains foresight, a cognitive and not a volitional state; or it might be argued that they should count as directly intended, since if a consequence is inseparable from an end it should count as part of the very same state of affairs as the desired outcome: in the case in point, blowing up the plane in flight just *is* killing the passengers, and a man should not be heard to say that he wanted the one but not the other. It is not necessary to inquire in which way Lord Hailsham would relate his terminology to Bentham's: what is clear is that if 'direct intention' is understood in this second way, then he can be said to be proposing that direct intent is necessary for murder.

There is little difficulty in applying the notion of direct intention, understood in this broad way, to the intention to kill or to cause grievous bodily harm. However, Lord Hailsham, while proposing a stricter requirement of directness of intent than his fellow judges proposed also a broader interpretation of the content of the intent: namely, that not only the intent to kill, or the intent to cause grievous bodily harm, but also the intent to expose a potential victim to the serious risk of death or grievous bodily harm, should suffice for malice aforethought in murder. The question at once arises: is the intent to expose to risk that is here in question a direct intent, or does an oblique intent suffice? I do not find it altogether easy to answer this question in the light of Lord Hailsham's speech.

In the case of a defendant 'who knows that a proposed course of conduct exposes a third party to a serious risk of death or grievous bodily harm without actually intending those consequences, but nevertheless and without lawful excuse deliberately pursues that course of conduct regardless', Lord Hailsham says, 'there is not merely actual foresight of the probable consequences but actual intention to expose his victim to the risk'. It is hard to see how this is necessarily so, unless 'intention' as it occurs at the end of this quotation means 'oblique intention'. Quoting with approval Lord Reid's dictum 'a man who deliberately shuts his eyes to the truth will not be heard to say that he did not know it', Lord Hailsham asks, 'Cannot the same be said of the state of intention of a man who, with actual appreciation of the risks and without lawful excuse, wilfully decides to expose potential victims to the risk of

death or really serious injury regardless of whether the consequences take place or not?' It is not at all clear what it would *be* to say
the same about direct intention: when what we are considering is a
volitional, not a cognitive state, what is the equivalent of shutting
one's eyes? It is presumably pretending not to want what one in
very truth does want. But a man who creates a risk of grievous
bodily harm by an unlawful act may *genuinely* not want to create
such a risk, in the sense that the creation of such a risk is neither an
end of his, nor a means he chooses to an end, nor an inevitable
consequence of such a means.[3] Of course, if Lord Hailsham in this
passage is talking about *oblique* intention, then the relevance of the
reference to shutting one's eye to the truth becomes clear.

Lord Hailsham claims that his proposal does not bring back the
doctrine of constructive malice, nor substitutes an objective for a
subjective test of intent:

> It simply proclaims the moral truth that if a man, in full knowledge
> of the danger involved, and without lawful excuse, deliberately does
> that which exposes a victim to the risk of the probable grievous
> bodily harm . . . or death, and the victim dies, the perpetrator of the
> crimes is guilty of murder and not manslaughter to the same extent
> as if he had actually intended the consequence to follow, and
> irrespective of whether he wishes it. This is because the two types of
> intention are morally indistinguishable, although factually and
> logically distinct. (p. 55)

The principal difficulty is in seeing what are the two types of
intention which are being claimed to be morally indistinguishable.
Is it being claimed that there is no moral difference between the
direct intention to do that which exposes a victim to the risk of
grievous bodily harm or death and the direct intention to kill? Such
a claim is surely extraordinary: any surgeon performing a difficult
operation has a direct intention 'to do that which exposes a victim
to the risk of grievous bodily harm or death'. (He does not, to be
sure, have a direct intention, in the strictest sense, 'to expose a
victim to the risk of grevious bodily harm – it is not a means or end

[3] The appellant in *Smith* v. *DPP* (1961) AC 290, for instance, if it is true that he 'merely
swerved or zigzagged' his car 'to shake off the officer' who was trying to arrest him, and was
horrified when he saw that he had caused the policeman to be run over.

of his that the operation should be risky, and he will welcome any procedure which will diminish its riskiness – but the periphrasis 'to do that which exposes' was obviously chosen with care, and for good reason.) It would be even more preposterous to claim that there was nothing morally to choose between the *oblique* intention to do that which creates a risk and the *direct* intention to kill or cause serious harm. We are left with the possibility that Lord Hailsham's contrast is between two oblique intentions: the oblique intention to create the risk, and the oblique intention to kill or seriously harm. But that cannot be the correct interpretation of the passage, for it would render otiose the careful argumentation of the first part of the speech to the effect that foresight of death or grievous bodily harm does not suffice for malice aforethought.

It is only when he comes to apply his test to the case in hand that Lord Hailsham finally makes it clear beyond doubt that the intention to create the risk of grievous bodily harm, to suffice for malice aforethought, must be direct. The case was one in which the appellant Hyam, out of jealousy of another woman *B* who had supplanted her in the affections of her paramour, went to *B*'s house in the early hours of the morning, poured petrol through the letter box, stuffed newspaper through it and lit it, then went home leaving the house burning with the result that *B*'s two daughters were suffocated. Her defence was that she had set fire to the house only in order to frighten *B* into leaving the neighbourhood. Lord Hailsham said:

> Once it is conceded that she was actually and subjectively aware of the danger to the sleeping occupants of the house in what she did . . . it must surely follow naturally that she did what she did with the intention of exposing them to danger of death or really serious injury regardless of whether such consequences actually ensued or not. Obviously in theory, a further logical step is involved after actual foresight of the probability of danger is established. But in practice and in the context of this case the step is not one which, given the facts, can be seriously debated. (p. 56)

If Lord Hailsham had been interested in the *oblique* intention to create a risk he could not have said that a further step was involved: for surely *no* step is involved in passing from 'I foresee that my actions make their death or serious injury probable' to 'I am aware that my actions are exposing them to a risk of death or serious injury.' The further step which Lord Hailsham mentions is the step between *seeing that* one is exposing to risk and *directly intending* to expose to risk. And surely he is right in saying that on the facts of this case there is no doubt that the intention as well as the foresight was present: as the appellant herself said, she wanted to frighten *B* into moving away from the neighbourhood; and the way she chose to frighten her was to put her and her family at serious risk.

But if we imagine the facts of the case slightly altered, an equally risky action might not have been an intentional placing at risk. Suppose that in order to vent her hatred of *B* Hyam had stolen all the love-letters and keepsakes exchanged between *B* and her own lover and had set them alight in *B*'s doorway with petrol; and suppose that the house had been burnt down as before and the children been killed. Here there would not necessarily have been any direct intention to set at risk. It is in a case such as this, it seems to me, that Lord Hailsham's *ratio decidendi* in *Hyam* would lead to an acquittal on a charge of murder, while the *ratio decidendi* of Lords Dilhorne and Cross of Chelsea would lead to a conviction (given that the accused realized it was highly probable that what she was doing would cause grievous bodily harm).

But we have not yet done justice to Lord Hailsham's full statement of his proposal. In answer to the question certified for appeal he put forward two propositions, of which the first runs:

> Before an act can be murder it must be 'aimed at someone' as explained in *Director of Public Prosecutions* v. *Smith* (1961) A.C. 290, 327, and must in addition be an act committed with one of the following intentions, the test of which is always subjective to the actual defendant:
> (1) The intention to cause death
> (2) The intention to cause grievous bodily harm . . .
> (3) Where the defendant knows that there is a serious risk that death or grievous bodily harm will ensue from his acts, and commits those acts deliberately and without lawful excuse, the intention to expose a potential victim to that risk as the result of those acts . . .
> (p. 58)

Here, in addition to one of the various forms of intention we have hitherto discussed, there are two further elements required for malice aforethought: that the acts which result in death should be committed 'without lawful excuse' and that they should be 'aimed at someone'. From various passages in his speech it is clear that Lord Hailsham's final formulation takes the shape it does because he wishes to exclude from the definition of murder both the surgeon who performs a high-risk operation and the motorist who kills on the road by dangerous driving, and because he wishes to include in the definition of murder the man who places a time-bomb in an aeroplane to recover the insurance on its cargo when it blows up in flight.

Lord Hailsham devotes considerable thought to the question of the surgeon's intention, and he seems to give two quite different reasons why on his definition a surgeon would be free of malice aforethought. Early in his discussion he says:

> The surgeon in a heart transplant operation may intend to save his patient's life, but he foresees as a high degree of probability that he will cause his death, which he neither intends nor desires, since he regards the operation not as a means to killing his patient, but as the best, and possibly the only, means of ensuring his survival. (p. 52)

One can say equally that just as the surgeon does not intend to cause death, he does not intend – directly – to cause a risk to life. Hence he will not have any of the intentions which are required, on Hailsham's test, for *mens rea*. But later in his speech the Lord Chancellor said that the reason why the heart surgeon, exposing his patient to the risk, is not guilty is because he is 'not exposing his patient to the risk without lawful excuse or regardless of the consequences'. This move seems both unnecessary and dangerous. It is unnecessary because once it is recognized that the surgeon does not directly intend the risk to the patient's life, there is no need to ask whether he has an excuse or not. It is dangerous, because if it is admitted that there can be a lawful excuse for intentionally creating a risk of life, the question must be raised what such excuses are and how far they extend: and Lord Hailsham, in marked contrast with the erudition he displayed on the topic of intent, did not feel it necessary, or did not find himself able, to quote a single case on the topic.

On the other hand, if we omit the proviso 'without lawful excuse' then it seems that the rather obscure phrase from *Smith* 'an unlawful and voluntary act aimed at someone' will be neither sufficient to catch the aeroplane time-bomber nor necessary to acquit the motor manslaughterer. The motor manslaughterer will already not be a murderer on the grounds that he has no intent to cause death, serious harm, or the risk of either; the aeroplane time-bomber will not be clearly caught because it is not clear that the act of putting a bomb on a cargo plane is 'aimed at someone'. This rather improbable person creates a problem precisely because he has no direct intent to kill or hurt anyone and 'aim' is a word which connotes, if any word does, directness of intent.

In spite of the difficulties and uncertainties, it seems to me that in proposing that direct intent rather than oblique be the test for *mens rea* in murder, and in introducing the notion of the wilful creation of a risk, Lord Hailsham has thrown a great deal of light on a confused and obscure area of English law. I wish to end this paper by suggesting a way in which Lord Hailsham's insights could be reformulated with certain modifications in a way which avoids the unclarities we have detected. But before doing so, I must turn for a while to the other main topic discussed by the House of Lords in *Hyam*, the content, not the directness of the intent: namely, whether for murder there was necessary an intent to kill (or to bring about a risk of death) or whether an intention to cause grievous bodily harm (or to bring about a risk of grievous bodily harm) sufficed.

Prior to *Hyam*, it had commonly been accepted that *R. v. Vickers* (1957) had established that, after, no less than before, the Homicide Act of 1957, killing with the intention to do some grievous bodily harm was murder. (There remained some degree of uncertainty about the precise nature of 'grievous' harm, which we can for our purposes ignore.) In a learned and keenly argued speech in *Hyam* Lord Diplock argued that *Vickers*, and *Smith* subsequently, had been wrong in allowing the intent to do grievous bodily harm as an alternative; they should have accepted the submission that in order to be guilty of murder an offender, if he did not intend to kill, must have intended or foreseen as a likely consequence of his act, that human life would be endangered. The decisions in those cases, he argued, were based on a misreading of the history of the doctrine of constructive malice from Lord Ellenborough's Act of 1803 (which made it a felony to wound people with intent to do them grievous bodily harm) right up to the Homicide Act of 1957 (which abolished the doctrine of constructive malice which had made it murder to kill in furtherance of a felony). The House of Lords should now overrule *Vickers* and *Smith* and take the opportunity, which had been lost in those cases, to restrict the relevant intention on a charge of murder to an intention to kill or to cause a bodily injury known to be likely to endanger life.

Lord Kilbrandon agreed in this with Lord Diplock. The majority, however, refused to overturn *Vickers*. Lord Hailsham said:

> If at this stage we were to overthrow the decision in *Vickers* a very high proportion of those now in prison for convictions of murder must necessarily have their convictions set aside and verdicts of manslaughter substituted. This consideration ought not perhaps logically to affect our decision, but I am personally relieved to find that I find myself in agreement with the decision in *Vickers*. (p. 46)

Apart from this consideration, which he very properly set aside, Lord Hailsham did not offer any argument in favour of the *Vickers* decision; and he admitted that 'technically this decision only rejected the ingenious argument of some academic lawyers that by enacting section 1 of the Homicide Act 1957, Parliament, despite the express words of the section, had inadvertently got rid of the doctrine of implied malice as well as constructive malice'. But of course if the intent to endanger life, and that alone, were allowed as an alternative to the intent to kill as *mens rea* for murder, then implied malice would remain a possibility.

Lord Dilhorne agreed with Lord Hailsham about the correctness of the decision in *Vickers*; but he drew attention to a paragraph in the 1953 report of the Royal Commission on Capital Punishment. 'We should therefore prefer to limit murder to cases where the act by which death is caused is intended to kill or to "endanger life" or is known to be likely to kill or endanger life' (p. 62). 'Our task', he went on, 'is to say what, in our opinion, the law is, not what it should be.' The intent to cause grievous bodily harm should therefore not be taken to be restricted to the intent to endanger life. 'To change the law to substitute "bodily injury known to the offender to be likely to cause death" for "grievous bodily harm" is a task that should, in my opinion, be left to Parliament if it thinks such a change expedient' (p. 62).

The third majority judge, Lord Cross of Chelsea, took an unusual course. He declared that he was unprepared to decide between the rival opinions of Lord Dilhorne and Lord Diplock about the correctness of *Vickers*. He went on: 'For my part, there-fore, I shall content myself with saying that on the footing that *R. v. Vickers* was rightly decided the answer to the question put to us should be "Yes" and that this appeal should be dismissed' (p. 63). I do not know what the precedents are for such conditional rulings. But to the layman it appears that whatever *Hyam* may have decided, one thing it did not decide was that *Vickers* was correct, since two judges thought it was, two though it was not, and one refused to say.[4]

Shortly after the decision in *Hyam* I wrote as follows:

> To the layman it seems a pity that the House of Lords did not combine the insights of both Lord Hailsham and Lord Diplock and define the *mens rea* required for murder as being the direct intention to kill or to create a serious risk of death. If, as Lords Diplock and Kilbrandon believed, and as Lord Cross of Chelsea professed himself willing to believe, it was open to the court to reverse *Vickers* and *Smith,* then in restricting the content of murderous intent to killing and endangering life the House would have made the law of murder take the form which, in the opinion of all of them, and of all who have tried to codify the English law of homicide, it *ought* to take. And in restricting the nature of *mens rea* to direct intention instead of allowing it to embrace foresight they would have brought greater conceptual clarity into the law and brought legal terminology more closely to common parlance.[5]

Further reflection on the speeches of the judges in *Hyam* has made me think that it is possible to argue that the case has actually

[4] I observe that the first question which follows the setting out of *Hyam* in the 1975 edition of Smith and Hogan's *Criminal Law: Cases and Materials* (Butterworth, 1975) is What is the status of Vickers? Is it binding on (i) trial judges? (ii) the Court of Appeal?' (p. 355).

[5] See above, pp. 13–14.

left the law in the state which I then described as a desirable position for which the opportunity has been lost. Because of the even division on the topic of *Vickers* it will be open for the House of Lords in future, and perhaps even for the Court of Appeal if not for a lower court, to rule against it. Because the *ratio decidendi* to which the Lord Chancellor appealed demanded that there should be direct and not oblique intention for malice aforethought, it will henceforth be open to an accused, who caused death by an act which he foresaw but did not intend to be likely to cause death, to plead that he lacked the necessary *mens rea* for a conviction of murder.

Whether or not this *is* the state of the law – and obviously that is in the end a question for the lawyer, not for the philosopher – I have no doubt it would be a good thing if it was. Murder would then be definable as doing an act which causes death with the intent either to kill or to create a serious risk of death: the intent in each case to be direct. The intent to kill should be taken to include the (direct) intent to bring about a state of affairs from which one knows death will certainly follow.

If this is the law, or if this were to become the law in England, that would be a significant change from the state which Hart, in the paper from which we began, regarded as a particularly fortunate one. I think that it would be a change for the better, not only because in cases of murder it would provide a simple and clear *ratio decidendi* which would accord with what Hart himself agrees to be the common man's notion of 'intention', but because it would be morally preferable to the state of the law as left by the Homicide Act, *Vickers* and *Smith*. The Law Commission said in 1967: 'In our view the essential element in murder should be willingness to kill, thereby evincing a total lack of respect for human life.' This seems to me correct. Unfortunately, the Law Commission's own definition of 'willingness to kill' was such as to make it tantamount to mere foresight of the likeliness of death: for it seems that if a man foresees death as a likely result of his actions, but does not therefore desist from his actions, he is willing for them to kill.[6] However, the Law Commission, like Lord Hailsham, was expressly anxious not

---

[6] See my 'Intention and Purpose in Law', p. 162.

to allow mere foresight to constitute the appropriate malice aforethought. The definition I have suggested enables us to capture the 'willingness to kill' which should be the essential element in murder in such a way that it does not collapse into mere foresight.

NOTE

In 1980 the Criminal Law Revision Committee published a report on Offences against the Person (Cmnd 7844). This report treated of the crime of murder, among other offences, and made various proposals for the reform of the law.

The Committee was dissatisfied with the common law concept of malice aforethought in the form which it had been left by *Hyam*. It took the decision as establishing that recklessness as well as intention sufficed for malice aforethought, and that the recklessness required need not concern causing death, but simply the causing of grievous bodily harm. Such a definition, the Report argued (paras 20–4), was far too wide to distinguish the cases of homicide that deserved to be singled out for the special stigma which attaches to the crime of murder.

In place of the definition, or definitions, to be gleaned from *Hyam*, the Committee recommended that it should only count as murder if the accused caused death with intent to kill, or caused death by an unlawful act intended to cause serious injury and known to the accused to involve a risk of causing death.

By 'intention' the Committee seems to have meant oblique intention; it included under this heading the state of mind of a person 'who, though he may not want the result to follow, knows that in the ordinary course of things it will do so'.

At the present time no steps have been taken to reform the law along the lines suggested by the Committee. In esence, therefore, the law of murder remains as it was determined by the decision in *Hyam*, with the complexities and ambiguities set out in the two preceding papers.

3

Duress *per Minas* as a Defence to Crime (1979)

I am honoured to be invited to reply to Lord Kilbrandon's paper on duress. The paper contains proposals of the highest interest for reform of the law. It is particularly interesting to hear these proposals from a noble and learned judge who has himself played an important part in the legal debate of the law of England on this topic. The present condition of that law, as he ably illustrates, is a very difficult one to justify. As Lord Kilbrandon modestly refuses to dwell on the judgments in which he took part, and as he assumed perhaps a greater familiarity with the cases in question than can be expected of the philosophers among his audience, I should like to spend some time on the present state of the law before considering the pros and cons of each of the proposals for reform.

First of all, it is commonly said in textbooks, and has from time to time been asserted judicially, that duress consisting in a serious threat to life and limb constitutes a defence in all except the most serious offences such as murder. Thus, the present Lord Chief Justice in the perjury case of *R.* v. *Hudson & Taylor*[1] said:

> It is clearly established that duress provides a defence in all offences including perjury (except possibly treason or murder as a principal) if the will of the accused has been overborne by threats of death or serious personal injury so that the commission of the alleged offence was no longer the voluntary act of the accused.

Lord Widgery's language is a little ambiguous: is he contrasting voluntary action with actions that are reflex, or somnambulistic, or gasping admissions of an exhausted man broken by torture, or does he mean by 'voluntary' actions unforced actions contrasting, say,

[1] [1971] 2 All ER 244.

with the reluctant action of a man sealing up a wad of £10 notes and putting them in an envelope to send to a blackmailer? It seems to be the common teaching of textbooks that actions under duress, even though they are voluntary in the first sense, are excusable if they fall short of involving crimes such as treason or murder. I am a little surprised to see Lord Kilbrandon apparently throwing doubt on the authority for this view. He writes:

> There are certainly to be found in the reports, though they are rare and not particularly impressive, cases other than murder cases in which duress has been held a complete exculpatory defence.

However, perhaps he is not here departing from the consensus about the existing law. Certainly, however, it seems that, if his reform proposals were accepted, the effect would be tightening-up of the law in respect of less serious crimes. For he seems to make no exceptions to the proposed rule that duress, if proved, should lead not to acquittal but to mitigation.

I do not myself find this proposal attractive. The present state of the law on duress as applied to less serious crimes, such as theft, seems to me to reflect a wholesome scale of values which regards human life as more important than the protection of property. As the law stands at present, a bank clerk will not be sent to prison for handing over cash to a gunman who threatens to kill him if he does not. If society does not want bank clerks to be obliged to defend their tills at the risk of their lives, I do not see why courts should send them to prison – even for a mitigated period – for not doing so. This, however, is a comparatively minor point. The really interesting and difficult question about duress is the question whether it should provide a defence or mitigation to a charge of murder.

In the case of *Lynch*,[2] the victim of the threats of the IRA gunmen, the three judges in the majority decided that duress was available as a defence to an accessory or principal in the second degree. They were hard put to it to find English authority for their view; they had to reject a large number of authorities that on the face of it told against them, and they could find in their favour nothing better than a dissenting judgment in the Supreme Court of

2 [1975] AC 653.

South Australia and a decision of a South African judge adminis-
tering Roman-Dutch law. Therefore, it was not the weight of legal
precedents which brought them to their decision: it was their
feeling that to exclude the defence of duress was unfair and
inhumane. As Lord Wilberforce put it, 'A law which requires
innocent victims of terrorist threats to be tried for murder and
convicted as murderers is an unjust law.' The arguments to this
effect can be reduced to two principal headings. The punishment of
killing under duress, it is claimed, is unjustified as retribution and
irrelevant as deterrent.

To punish people who have killed under threat to their own life,
it is argued, is to demand a degree of heroism which the law has no
right to exact from the ordinary citizen. In the words of Lord
Morris, 'The law must take a commonsense view and remember
that the instinct and perhaps the duty of self-preservation is
powerful and natural.'

The infliction of punishment on those convicted of crimes is most
commonly justified by the deterrent effect of the threat of punishment. But no threat which the law can make will weigh more with a
man than his immediate and overriding desire to save his life from
instant attack. The punishment of crimes committed under duress,
therefore, goes against the principle of economic deterrence and
should be abandoned in any humane legislature.

I have stated these arguments against excluding duress as a
defence in general terms as applying to murder, whether committed as principal, or as accessory. In the case of *Lynch*, of course, the
arguments were stated with reference only to killing as principal in
the second degree, and their Lordships took pains not to commit
themselves on the topic of murder as a whole. But as two of the
majority judges pointed out, when they found themselves in a
minority in the case of *Abbott* in which duress was pleaded as a
defence to a murder charge by an actual killer, the arguments had
equal force in either case.

In the minority in *Lynch* were Lord Kilbrandon and Lord Simon
of Glaisdale. Lord Kilbrandon agreed with the majority judges that
there was something inhumane in refusing to allow duress as a
defence or mitigation, but he thought that the law as it stood clearly
took this inhumane view and it was not for five Lords of Appeal but

for Parliament to change the law in a more humane direction. Lord Simon, while agreeing that any change in the law was a matter for Parliament, thought there was rather more to be said for the law as it stood.

The case for the existing law was put most eloquently by Lord Salmon for the majority in the later Privy Council case of *Abbott*.[3] To allow duress as a defence to killers, he said, might prove to be a charter for terrorists, gangleaders and kidnappers:

> A terrorist of notorious violence might e.g. threaten death to *A* and his family unless *A* obeys his instructions to put a bomb with a time fuse set by *A* in a certain aircraft, and/or in a thronged market, railway station or the like. *A*, under duress, obeys his instructions and as a result, hundreds of men, women and children are killed or mangled. Should the contentions made on behalf of the appellant be correct, *A* would have a complete defence, and, if charged, would be bound to be acquitted and set at liberty. Having now gained some real experience and expertise, he might again be approached by the terrorist who would make the same threats and exercise the same duress under which *A* would then give a repeat performance killing even more men, women and children. Is there any limit to the number of people you may kill to save your own life and that of your family?

The joint effect, then, of *Lynch* and *Abbot* is that duress is now available as a defence to murder if the accused is not the actual killer, but is not available if he is a principal in the first degree. I agree with Lord Kilbrandon that this is an unsatisfactory state of affairs because the distinction between principal and accessory in English law is not clear enough or strong enough to bear the weight which judges put upon it. To remedy the situation Lord Kilbrandon has two proposals. One is that the crime of murder should be abolished and should be merged, along with manslaughter, in a new crime called unlawful homicide. The second is that duress, like provocation, would be available not as an absolute defence but as one which will lead to mitigation of sentence. If the crime of murder is to remain, then duress should be a plea leading to a reduction from murder to manslaughter.

[3] [1977] AC 755.

The proposal to abolish the crime of murder seems to me an attractive one only if we are sure that the death penalty will never be reintroduced. In present circumstances, when the reintroduction of the death penalty seems a possibility which is not at all remote, it seems to me desirable to continue to try to separate out a particular class of unlawful homicide as constituting an offence of unparalleled seriousness. But I do not wish to enter upon this argument in the present paper, but rather to consider Lord Kilbrandon's proposal in its more modest form.

Before doing so I should like to say something about one more recent case which is not mentioned by Lord Kilbrandon, *The Queen* v. *Charles Anthony Fitzpatrick* in the Northern Ireland Court of Criminal Appeal.[4] In this case the appellant was a young man who will sitting for A-levels joined the IRA believing a civil war to be imminent. He was trained in the use of firearms and carried out vigilante duty in the Antrim Road. But because his studies suffered he wanted to go away to England and asked to be released from the IRA. He was told by an IRA officer that if he left the country his parents would be shot and he was ordered to take part in a bank robbery. During the robbery he shot and killed a banker who tried to stop him. He was found guilty of murder and robbery. The defence of duress was offered, but the judge held that, having joined the IRA and voluntarily exposed himself to the risk of compulsion by the IRA to commit crimes on its behalf, the appellant was not entitled to rely on the defence of duress exercised by that organization. The judgment of the trial judge was upheld by the Court of Criminal Appeal.

I understand that leave to appeal to the House of Lords against the decision in *Fitzpatrick* was refused by the Court of Criminal Appeal. If we assume, however, that the law in England on this point is the same as that in Northern Ireland as decided in *Fitzpatrick*, we have the following overall law on the topic of duress. First, duress which is itself voluntary excuses from all crimes except murder by an actual killer. Second, duress which is the result of a voluntary action does not excuse from robbery and, therefore, presumably not from the more serious crime of murder. (In the *Fitzpatrick* case it was not suggested that the actual shooting was

---

[4] Unreported. I am indebted to Mr C. McCrudden for drawing this case to my attention.

under duress, but only the robbery in the course of which the shot was fired.)

I am not sure whether Lord Kilbrandon would wish voluntary duress to be excluded from his proposal that duress should be a mitigating circumstance. In his remarks in *Lynch* he noted that an exclusion of voluntary duress was to be found in the codes of most jurisdictions which admitted duress as an excuse. He said, 'Such a provision figures in the codes; I do not see how it could become part of English law save by legislation.' It does, in fact seem to have become part of Northern Irish law without legislation; but perhaps Lord Kilbrandon would regard Lord Chief Justice Lowry's decision as being as much a usurpation of the functions of Parliament as the majority judgment in *Lynch*.

Such is the state of the law. Like Lord Kilbrandon I regard it as unsatisfactory. In particular there is an illogicality in the different attitudes which the law takes to duress and which it takes to necessity. As Lord Kilbrandon says, legal authorities distinguish necessity from duress on the ground that the latter is an instance of compulsion by human, the former by natural forces. The case of *R.* v. *Dudley & Stephens*,[5] in which the shipwrecked mariners killed and ate the ship's boy, laid down that necessity did not entitle a man to take innocent life. Majority judges in *Lynch* do not seem to have regarded themselves as overruling *Dudley & Stephens*. It seems therefore that duress will sometimes excuse the killing of the innocent, but necessity never will. This is strange, as the case for disallowing duress as a defence is stronger than that for disallowing necessity.

There were, as I have shown, two principal arguments in favour of allowing the defence of duress: that it demanded heroism to give up one's own life rather than to take another, and that the deterrent effect of the threat of punishment would be neutralized in circumstances of duress. The argument for disallowing the defence of duress was that to allow it was to enable a gangleader to confer impunity on any of his subordinates whom he terrified sufficiently. The two arguments in favour of allowing duress are equally arguments in favour of allowing necessity; the argument against it does not apply in the case of necessity.

To my mind it seems that the way out of the illogicalities of the

[5] [1881–5] All ER Ref. 61.

present situation is not the one proposed by Lord Kilbrandon. It is rather to overrule *Lynch*. The arguments used in *Abbott* and *Fitzpatrick* seem to me basically sound and those used by the majority in *Lynch* to be specious. Let us take first the question of moral culpability. It is true that to resist duress, or to refrain from taking life under necessity, may call for heroism. It does not follow that it is morally permissible to do anything else. Most of us most of the time can steer a middle course between wickedness and heroism, but in tragic circumstances – as for instance in concentration camps or in a natural disaster – we may be faced with a stark choice between the two. If the law punishes immoral actions done under duress or necessity then it is not being unjust or enforcing anything beyond minimum standards of morality. But of course, while it is a necessary condition for an action to be severely punishable by law that it should be an immoral action, it is not a sufficient condition; and to point out that killing an innocent person to save one's own life is wicked does not yet establish whether it should be a crime.

To settle this we need to consider the second of the arguments in favour of allowing duress, the argument about the inefficacy of punishment. This argument, it seems to me, fails to take account of the fact that law is itself a system of threats. Law and duress are, as it were, in the same business. In the words of Stephen[6] quoted in *Abbott*:

> Criminal law is itself a system of compulsion on the widest scale. It is a collection of threats of injury to life, liberty, and property if people do commit crimes. Are such threats to be withdrawn as soon as they are encountered by opposing threats? The law says to a man intending to commit murder, If you do it I will hang you. Is the law to withdraw its threat if someone else says, If you do not do it I will shoot you?
>
> Surely it is at the moment when temptation to crime is strongest that the law should speak most clearly and emphatically to the contrary.

If this argument is correct, as I think it is, it tells not only against allowing necessity and duress as defences, but also against allowing them as mitigations. In fact, if we were to consider nothing but

[6] J. F. Stephen, *A History of the Criminal Law of England*, (Macmillan, 1883) p. 107.

deterrence alone, the conclusion to be drawn would surely be that crimes committed under duress should be more severely punished than normal crimes, since a more severe threat of punishment will be necessary to counterbalance the threats constituting the duress. If it be said that whatever penalty the law provides can always be matched by a sufficiently ruthless criminal, this might be met by allowing judges discretion, above a certain minimum, to add ever greater and more terrifying refinements of punishment to whatever threat had been made on a particular occasion. If we reject this bizarre suggestion, it is not because we regard deterrence as irrelevant to actions under duress but because we know deterrence must be mitigated by humanity.

But if humanity towards the criminal tells against increasing the penalities for crimes committed under duress, humanity towards the victims of criminals – actual and potential – tells against mitigating them. When the majority judges in *Lynch* said that 'law which requires innocent victims of terrorists to be tried for murder and convicted as murderers is an unjust law', they begged the question by using the word *innocent*; and the sufferings of the indisputably innocent – the general public – seem likely to be increased rather than diminished by adopting a lenient policy towards crimes committed under duress. For, to the extent that duress is a defence to murder, the discipline exercised over their associates by sufficiently ruthless gangleaders or terrorist chieftains is to that degree reinforced.

There will, of course, be particular cases in which the incarceration for life of one who has killed under duress or out of necessity would be inhumane and unnecessary. In such cases the executive can exercise the powers available to it to temper the sentences passed by the courts, as it did in the classic case of *Dudley & Stephens*. But the mitigation of sentence should not be something which can be counted on in advance by someone who is tempted to give in to threats and take innocent life. It is a very great misfortune to be placed in a situation where one must kill and suffer the consequences, or be killed oneself: any man must pray never to be thus placed between the devil and the deep blue sea. But if the law takes away the deep blue sea, a man will go wherever the devil drives.

4

The Expert in Court
(1982)

Whenever a particularly horrific murder is committed, or whenever a public figure is successfully or unsuccessfully attacked by an assassin, there is great public interest not only in the crime but in the trial and in the procedures of the trial. It is indeed through newspaper reports of the trials of the accused in spectacular crimes that the general public acquires most of its knowledge of the operation of the laws and the procedures of the courts. During 1982, public interest was focused on the defence of insanity and related matters on both sides of the Atlantic, in England by the trial of the 'Yorkshire Ripper', Peter Sutcliffe, and in the United States by the trial of John Hinckley, the would-be assassin of President Reagan.

The concern took different forms on the different sides of the Atlantic. The condemnation of Sutcliffe was probably generally popular with the public, but caused concern among lawyers and psychiatrists; the acquittal of Hinckley, while defended by a number of those professionally concerned with the work of the courts, was widely regarded by the public as showing that there was a crying need to reform the law. The *Sutcliffe* case does not, considered in itself, give rise to calls for the reform of the English law of homicide; those who considered the verdict of guilty unjust thought that justice could have been done if the defence had been allowed to plead diminished responsibility in accordance with the Homicide Act 1957. I shall later offer some observations on the diminished responsibility defence; but I shall take as my starting point not the trial of Sutcliffe but that of Hinckley.

There was no question that Hinckley had shot the President, and that he had intended to kill him: the defence lawyers had to establish that he suffered from a mental illness which was so severe that he 'lacked substantial capacity to appreciate the wrongfulness of his conduct and could no longer control his own conduct'. Hinckley had a history of inadequate performance and feckless conduct, which had led to his being referred to psychiatrists on several occasions. On the last of these the psychiatrists offered the advice that his parents should cease to take responsibility for his upkeep, and turn him onto the world to take care of himself. At the trial Dr Carpenter, the psychiatrist called as a defence witness who was an expert on schizophrenia, said that this cutting off by his parents severed Hinckley's last links with the real world. Hinckley fell in love with a young actress, Jodie Foster. On the one occasion when he was able to meet her, she rebuffed him. He wrote to her later that he was going to make an attempt on Reagan's life 'because I just cannot wait to impress you'. He did, in due course, make the attempt; it was unsuccessful, and he was imprisoned and tried for attempted assassination. At the trial, the decisive evidence was that of a series of psychiatrists. As Hinkley later described it, 'The defence doctors found me to be delusional, psychotic, schizophrenic and perhaps the most alienated young man they have ever examined. On the other hand, despite evidence to the contrary, the prosecution doctors said I merely had some personality problems and deserved to be punished with imprisonment.'

Before the trial Hinckley was examined for four months by psychiatrists; their medical reports were filed in July 1981 and he came up for trial in May 1982. The chief defence psychiatrist, Dr Carpenter, testified that Hinckley suffered from 'process schizophrenia', i.e. slowly developing schizophrenia; he testified that while Hinckley knew that shooting Reagan was illegal he did not appreciate what he was doing. 'In his mental state . . . [the victims] were bit players, and were not, of themselves, important.' Prosecution witnesses denied that Hinckley was suffering from schizophrenia. In July 1982 the jury, to the astonishment of the greater part of the nation, acquitted Hinckley on grounds of insanity. He was committed to the secure hospital in Washington DC from which, a few weeks later, he wrote a jaunty article in *Newsweek* defending the role of the insanity defence in the American legal system. *Newsweek* pointed out a paradox to which his commitment led. Once he was committed, it was open to his attorneys to argue that he should be released because he was no longer mentally ill. In support of this claim they could point to the testimony of the prosecution throughout the trial. The government lawyers, on the other hand, in order to ensure that he continued to be hospitalized, would have to appeal to the eloquent speeches of the defence lawyers to the effect that the accused was severely mentally ill.

Many in the United States felt that the outcome of the Hinckley trial was outrageous. Among those who felt like this, not unnaturally, was President Reagan. In late September 1982 he announced that a new legislative package sent to Capitol Hill would include '"common sense" revision of the insanity defence, a defence that has been much misinterpreted and abused'. A number of states have effectively abolished the insanity defence in recent times, and others have been reported to be considering doing so in future, in effect. Thus, in the states of Michigan, Indiana and Illinois an accused with a record like that of Hinckley could be found 'guilty but mentally ill'; he would receive the same sentence as a sane person but would, in theory if not often in practice, start serving the sentence in hospital and be transferred to prison only after being cured of his mental illness. In Idaho the law concerning the treatment of insane defendants is even stricter. In general, the reaction of those in the United States disquieted by the Hinckley verdict has been to call for revision of the insanity defence, as for the quite different reasons the Sutcliffe trial here led to worry about its relation to the defence of diminished responsibility. There may be good grounds for doing this, which I shall look at later. But I believe the correct starting point for a reform suggested by the outcome of these trials is at a level of greater generalization: it is to look at the role played, in the Anglo-American legal system, by the expert witnesses.

As all textbooks on evidence tell us, the foundation of the rules governing expert evidence was, in the words of Lawton LJ in *R.* v. *Turner* 'laid by Lord Mansfield in *Folkes* v. *Chadd* (1782) 3 Doug. 157 and was well laid: the opinion of scientific men upon proven facts may be given by men of science within their own science'.[1] These words, though often quoted and attributed to Lord Mansfield, do not occur in his judgment; but they accurately summarize

[1] [1975] QB 834, 841.

its gist and they have served often as the basis of the practice of courts in the admission of expert evidence.

The justification of the admission of expert evidence is clear. There are many matters of specialized knowledge which are relevant to matters at issue before the courts, on which the courts would be unable, unless aided by experts, to reach a correct conclusion. It is sometimes said – and the classical formulation suggests this – that the admissibility of expert evidence is an exception to non-admissibility of opinion evidence. But it is clear that expert opinion is not the mere conjecture, surmise or speculation of the expert: it is his judgment on a matter of fact; it differs from ordinary evidence on matters of fact in that it is not based on the use of untutored senses or on the observation of the average man, but on specialized training, experience out of the common, and/or theoretical information of a recondite kind.

There are many cases in practice in which it is clear that a court needs and benefits from expert opinion. Is the silting in a harbour caused by an embankment?[2] Are certain documents in the defendant's handwriting or not?[3] Was the plaintiff suffering from lead poisoning?[4] Were certain marks on the accused's clothing bloodstains?[5] What is the proper rent for a property of a certain size in a certain area?[6] The appropriate experts, giving evidence on such matters, can very reasonably be described as men of science offering an opinion within their own science.

The classical formulation of the role of the expert witness, however, is bound to raise a query in the mind of anyone who has received a philosophical training. What, we may wonder, counts as a science? It seems clear we must know the boundaries of science, if we are to know who is a man of science, and if we are to tell when he is talking within his science, and when he goes beyond its limits. And the question 'What is a science?' is a philosophical question, and a very old one: it occupied Plato for most of his life. But the question, though philosophical, is far from being an abstract one

---

[2] *Folkes* v. *Chadd* (1782) 3 Doug. 157.
[3] *R.* v. *Silverlock* [1894] 2 QB 766.
[4] *Ramsay* v. *Watson* (1961) 108 CLR 642.
[5] *Anderson* v. *The Queen* [1972] AC 100.
[6] *English Exporters (London) Ltd* v. *Eldonwall Ltd* [1973] Ch. 415.

with no consequences for practice in the law. How, and by whom, is it decided that a discipline is one where expertise may justly be claimed? How and by whom is it decided when an expert in a scientific discipline is expressing an opinion on matters within his science? Who decides when he ceases to do so, and is expressing no longer an expert opinion but merely the opinion of an expert? How and by whom *should* these questions be decided in a rational system of jurisprudence?

I have been able to find remarkably little discussion of these questions in the textbooks I have consulted and in the articles to which I have been referred. In one way this was disappointing: in another it was encouraging. It appears that the questions are still, in law, open ones to be argued from first principles; questions therefore on which it may be possible for a philosopher to throw light even in the company of lawyers.

Given that a certain discipline is a science, there is a considerable amount of authority about what a person must do or be in order to count as a man of science.

On the one hand, he need not have any formal qualification (for engineers, for instance, there were no formal qualifications until recently) nor need he have acquired his expertise in his profession. The leading case here is *R. v. Silverlock*.[7] In that case the solicitor for the prosecution was called as an expert witness: he had given ten years study to handwriting, and was invited to testify that certain documents were in the defendant's handwriting. It was objected that he had not acquired his knowledge in the course of his business, and so was not an expert. The objection was overruled; correctly, according to Lord Russell on appeal: 'It is true that the witness who is called upon to give evidence founded on a comparison of handwritings must be *peritus*; he must be skilled in doing so; but we cannot say he must have become *peritus* in the way of his business or in any definite way. The question is, is he *peritus*? Is he skilled? Has he an adequate knowledge?'

On the other hand, it is also clear that a person is not entitled to give expert evidence if his only knowledge is acquired in the courts of the actual case[8] or is simply based on hearsay regarding

---

[7] [1894] 2 QB 766.
[8] *R. v. Crouch* (1850) 11 Cox CC 546.

transactions similar to those before the court.[9] Within these limits, the degree of his competence will be established in his evidence in chief, and will be tested at that time by cross-examination. Once it is established thus that he possesses the minimum of skill for his evidence to be admissible, the jury will then decide what weight to attach to it in accordance with the degree of skill which they believe him to possess.

It is not necessary, then, in order for a discipline to be an admissible expertise, that it should be an academically or professionally organized branch of study with formal qualifications. But the more important, and more difficult question is this: if a formal organization is not necessary for a discipline to constitute a 'science', is it sufficient for purposes of expert evidence? Must the courts recognize as a science everything alleged to be one, or which a would-be expert witness presents as one, or can they take cognizance of the existence of disciplines which are sciences in appearance and not in reality? If they cannot, then must they not be the victims of every sufficiently imposing charlatan? If they can, how are they best to do so?

It cannot be pretended that in different societies, or within the same society, there will be agreement, even among the most educated sections of the society, about which disciplines are genuine sciences and which are pseudo-sciences. I do not know whether, in any state of the Commonwealth, or of the United States, expert evidence has been admitted from astrologers or witchdoctors: evidence, I mean, not simply about the beliefs of those who believe in astrology or witchcraft, but about matters of substance, as whether an accused was under the influence of astral forces, or whether his victim had placed him under a spell. But there is no need to travel abroad to find examples of would-be sciences which are regarded with suspicion by persons of learning and wisdom. In our own society, the question whether the social sciences deserve the name of 'science' has been ventilated by some at the very highest level of the educational hierarchy. I do not know whether sociologists are admitted frequently in our courts as expert witnesses; in the famous case of *Lowery* v. *The Queen*[10] an educational

---

[9] *English Exporters (London) Ltd* v. *Eldonwall Ltd* [1973] Ch. 415.
[10] [1974] AC 85.

psychologist was admitted, and this no doubt frequently happens in cases which have acquired less notoriety.

There is a discipline which is at present developing named 'stylometry'. It consists in the statistical study of features of literary style, such as vocabulary choice, word and sentence length, syntactic constructions, collocations of words and parts of speech. One of its most interesting applications is to authorship attribution studies. It is possible to detect in the writings of individual authors statistical regularities – usually of rather humble and uninteresting kinds – which are characteristic of their style. Works which are doubtfully attributed to authors can be studied and examined to see if they possess those features which characterize the undoubtedly authentic works. If they do, and if the writings of other suggested authors do not, this provides an argument in favour of authenticity. If they do not, and all the genuine works of the alleged authors do, this provides an argument against authenticity. Stylometric arguments of this kind have been applied to a number of well-known problems of authorship attribution in recent years, and stylometrists claim to have solved long-standing disputes. Did St Paul write the Pastoral Epistles? No, suggest Grayson and Herdan. Did he write the Captivity Epistles? No, proclaims A. Q. Morton. Who wrote the Junius letters? Sir Philip Francis, say most scholars: and Alvar Ellegård has produced striking statistical arguments in their favour. Who wrote the disputed Federalist papers? According to Mosteller and Wallace, the odds are well over 80 to 1 that Madison wrote them all. Who wrote *The Boke of Sir Thomas More*? William Shakespeare, says T. Merriam. Did one person write Genesis? Yes, says Y. Radday.

Stylometry is a new and modest discipline. That is to say, it is a new discipline, and it ought to be a modest one. Not all its practitioners, I fear, in claims to scientific standing, have been as modest as they should. It is only since the Second World War that stylometry has been a self-conscious discipline. To make it at all attractive or efficient as a general field of study scholars had to wait for the development of sampling theory and the availability of computers to make concordances and to carry out the statistical calculations. There are perhaps 100 people throughout the world at present working on authorship attribution studies, who meet at

46	Philosophy and Law

conferences under the aegis of such bodies as the Association for Literary and Linguistic Computing, and publish papers – not always without difficulty – in learned journals.

It is my belief that stylometry, and in particular stylometric authorship attribution, is a genuine science and not a pseudo-science. I believe that it should be able to provide genuine arguments for and against particular attributions. I should indeed declare an interest in the subject, since I have written one book,[11] in which I claim to have solved by stylometric methods an ancient, though not very important, problem about the provenance of some of Aristotle's ethical writings; and I have written another book as an elementary introduction to statistics[12] for students of literature who wish to pursue stylometric studies but lack, as I do, any but the most elementary mathematical training. So it is with a prejudice for, rather than against, stylometry, that I approach the question whether it is a fit subject for expert evidence.

A. Q. Morton, one of the earliest and most eloquent of those who applied stylometric tests to ancient Greek texts, was also the first stylometrist to be called as an expert witness to test the authenticity of an alleged confession to a police officer, made in accordance with the Judges' Rules. I quote his own words: 'The case which established the legal precedent in England came to the author in 1974 when a letter asking for help arrived from Steven Raymond who was, as he put it, confined in a prison of stone by a tissue of lies.'[13] There were 11 police statements containing words attributed to him; seven of these he accepted as genuine, four he rejected as fabricated; if they were, the prosecution's case would be destroyed. The genuine material ran to 2200 words, the rejected 1100; the two letters he had written for help contained 2200 words and 2100 words, so that five genuine samples could be compared with one disputed one. By studying features such as the proportion of occurrences of 'the' preceded by 'of' or the number of times 'and' occurs as the first word of a sentence, Morton cast doubt on the genuineness of the disputed confession.

[11] *The Aristotelian Ethics* (Oxford University Press, 1978).
[12] *The Computation of Style* (Pergamon, 1982).
[13] *Literary Detection* (1980) p. 204.

On this evidence the accused was found not guilty of all charges in which the disputed statements were cited (he got a short sentence for other offences). The legal precedent had been established with some success. But some aspects of the case are less than satisfactory. The evidence was laid before the prosecuting counsel in court and the proceedings were adjourned for ten minutes to allow him to absorb the opinion and the evidence on which it was based. This could only be fair to a counsel who was highly numerate. That it was unfair to the advantage of the accused is some consolation.[14]

The consolation was not very great, in the light of the sequel. Two years later the BBC wished to make a programme about the Judges' Rules and connected topics: it was thought that Raymond might be a useful person to interview. He could not be traced. A report in *The Daily Telegraph*[15] suggested a reason why. He was being held in Zurich on suspicion of involvement in the Heathrow Airport strongroom theft in June 1976.

The tests which Morton used to cast doubt on Raymond's confession may indeed be valuable methods of acquiring evidence about authenticity. But they had not been sufficiently tried for their use in court to be justified. On Morton's own account, when he started to work on the *Raymond* case he had no previous experience of working on English stylometry. In his book Morton uses similar tests to show how the parts of *Sanditon* which were written by Jane Austen can be discriminated from those parts written by a skilled twentieth-century imitator. Morton's statistics for the genuine Jane Austen are based on a sample of five chapters (a sample of size comparable to the genuine Raymond sample). L. Burnard, of the Oxford Computing Centre, has shown that if Morton's discriminators are tried on the whole of the genuine corpus, many genuine chapters appear spurious. In my opinion, to this day the type of test proposed by Morton and his followers such as Merriam, has not yet been sufficiently validated to be an appropriate subject for expert testimony in the courts.

The United States courts have not, so far, followed the precedent set in the English courts in the *Raymond* case. When Patricia Hearst

---

[14] Ibid., p. 208.
[15] 22 April 1977.

was tried for bank robbery an important part of the evidence consisted of tape-recorded revolutionary statements spoken by members of the Symbionese Liberation Army. Hearst's counsel, F. Lee Bailey, challenged the attribution of these statements to the accused, and sought leave to introduce expert 'psycholinguistic' testimony on the issue of authorship. The trial judge ruled against admitting the testimony, saying that an aura of special reliability might have attached to the expert's testimony which would have been unjustified in view of 'the relative infancy of this area of scientific endeavour'. In my view the judge acted wisely. Stylometry may well in due course be established as a science; all that can so far be claimed is that it is an area of scientific endeavour.

Humane studies – the study of letters and works of art – are contrasted with science. If we are to restrict the scope of expert evidence to the strict field of science, we would have to exclude men of letters and critics of works of art. But the Obscene Publications Act 1959 states 'It is hereby declared that the opinion of experts as to the literary, artistic, scientific or other merits of an article may be admitted in any proceedings under this Act either to establish or to negative'[16] the ground that publication is for the public good in the interests of literature, art or learning. Thus, by this Act, literary and aesthetic criticism are placed on a level with science as objects of expertise.

Finally, one may ask whether matters of morality – for instance, the tendency of an object to deprave and corrupt – can be regarded as something on which expert opinion might assist the courts. Yes, answered the Lord Chief Justice in the court of Queen's Bench in the case of *DDP* v. *A. and B.C. Chewing Gum Ltd.*[17] In that case the defendants were charged with contravening the Obscene Publications Act 1959 by publishing for gain 43 obscene bubble gum battle cards, for sale to children of five years and over. The question submitted to the court was whether the evidence of child psychiatrists had been rightly excluded at first instance, on the ground that it was evidence on the very issue the court has to determine, which was generally excluded by a long-standing rule of common law. Lord Parker CJ said:

[16] s. 4 (2).
[17] [1968] 1 QB 159.

With the advance of science more and more inroads have been made into the old common law principles. Those who practise in the criminal courts see every day cases of experts being called on the question of diminished responsibility, and although technically the final question 'Do you think he was suffering from diminished responsibility?' is strictly inadmissible, it is allowed time and time again without any objection.[18]

The sciences of mind are no doubt less exact than those of the body; but still it is quite proper – at least in the case of children – to ask psychiatrists what the effect on the minds of children of different groups would be if certain types of photographs were put before them; and though it would be wrong to ask the direct question whether any particular cards tended to deprave and corrupt, that being a matter for the trier of fact, the defence would be allowed to put it to the witness that a particular card could not corrupt, in order to get an answer 'No' from the expert.

We have clearly come some way from Lord Mansfield's dictum. 'Men of science' now include not only natural scientists, but also aesthetic critics and the experts, whoever they may be, on depravity and corruption. Can these be said to be scientists, to be appropriately called as experts?

What are the criteria for deciding whether something is or is not a science? Any philosopher would tremble at the prospect of giving a simple answer to such a question; but I shall hardily venture four criteria which are necessary conditions for a discipline to be scientific.

First, the discipline must be consistent. That is to say, different experts must not regularly give conflicting answers to questions which are central to their discipline. That is not to say that there may not be differences of opinion between experts. In any science there will be such differences on matters which the differing experts will each regard as difficult or borderline cases. In a case which each expert agrees to be paradigm instance of a phenomenon falling under the explanatory principles of the discipline, there will not be disagreement unless there is disagreement about the existince or non-existence of the evidence for the phenomenon.

[18] Ibid., p. 164.

Secondly, the discipline must be methodical. That is to say, there will be agreement about the appropriate procedures for gathering information within the discipline. A procedure carried out by one expert to reach a particular conclusion is one which must be capable of duplication by any other expert. This does not mean that every set of results which *A* produces must be capable of replication by *B*, but if the results are not repeated there must be agreement between members of the discipline as to what kind of explanation of the failure is appropriate.

Thirdly, the discipline must be cumulative. That is to say, though any expert must be able to repeat the results of others he does not have to: he can build upon foundations that others have built. The findings of one generation of workers in the discipline are not called in question by the workers of the next (that is not to say that they may not be placed in an altered context, or accounted for by a higher-level system of explanation; this quite frequently happens). But research, once done, does not need doing again; if you have to repeat someone else's experiments, or resample his population, on the very same issue as him, that shows you think there was something wrong with his experiment, or something faulty in his sampling.

Finally, the discipline must be predictive and therefore falsifiable. It need not necessarily predict the future (palaeontology does not). But it must predict the not yet known from the already known (as the doctor's diagnosis of the nature of a terminal illness predicts what will be found at the post mortem, and is falsified if it proves otherwise). This is sometimes taken as the hallmark of a scientific discipline, but wrongly. A system for picking lucky numbers in a lottery may be predictive, and not only falsifiable, but very regularly falsified, while being no science for all that.

It is clear from this that a number of disciplines in which we have considered the appropriateness of expert evidence do not pass the test. Stylometry is not consistent or methodical. That is to say, it is not yet: but there are very good hopes that it may be. It is an infant science, not a pseudo science. Literary criticism, on the other hand, though it may be consistent (there is wide agreement, at least about the past, which writers are great, and for what reasons) is only doubtfully methodical, and it is certainly not cumulative. Critics of one age do not regard themselves as casting doubt on the critics of an earlier age when they propose fresh readings of the classics; a modern Shakespearean critic will neither agree with Johnson or Bradley nor necessarily think they botched their work. One cannot say of criticism, as one can say of research, that if it is once well done it does not need doing again. Literary criticism, again, is not predictive; there is no clear way of proving a critic's reading right or wrong; no outcome which will test his predictions. For these reasons literary and artistic criticism is highly vulnerable to fashion. It is interesting to reread, a few years later, the evidence of the 'experts' who testified at the trial of *Lady Chatterley*. It has already acquired a period flavour greater than that of testimony given by ballistics experts and toxicologists testifying 50 years ago.

The decision whether something is or is not a science is, I have said, a matter for philosophy. Philosophy itself is clearly, by the test I have suggested, no science. It is neither consistent, methodological, cumulative or predictive. The difficulty of deciding in the courtroom whether something is a science is not a difficulty which could be solved by admitting philosophers into the courtroom as higher order experts.

As matters stand in courts in common law jurisdictions the question whether a discipline is a science capable of being the subject of expert evidence is something which has to be fought out in the courts in the context of a particular case. One party will seek to bring forward the evidence of X, an expert in science S; the other party may question, not the particular competence of X, but the genuineness or objectivity of science S. The judge in deciding whether to admit the evidence of the expert has to decide, *inter alia*, whether the discipline in which he practises is a genuine field of expertise. Until a science is well established, such a decision may have to be settled afresh from case to case. Now no doubt judicial notice may be taken of the fact that astronomy is a science and that fingerprints are a reliable method of identification; but neither judge nor jury within the course of an ordinary trial can be put in possession of the relevant evidence for deciding whether psychoanalysis is a science, nor whether stylometry is a reliable method of settling the authenticity of documents. However much we may be convinced of the merits of the Anglo-Saxon judicial system, the courtroom is not the best place, and the adversary procedure is not the right method, to decide what is and what is not a science.

In the light of what we have said we shall turn to the question: is psychiatry a science? The answer, in one sense, may seem obvious. Medicine is a paradigm case of a science; psychiatrists are all medical men; therefore psychiatrists are men of science. And it is absolutely clear that there are, and will be, many occasions on which the courts cannot proceed without the advice of psychiatrists on how to treat those who come up before them for trial and for sentencing.

On the other hand it cannot be said that psychiatry, as it appears in the courts, displays the lineaments of a science as I have described them. It is a common sight to see highly respected psychiatrists contradicting each other's diagnoses, and that not in rare or difficult cases, but cases which are typical of the disturbed offenders who come before the courts. Moreover the profession itself seems to be in serious doubt about some of the major concepts of the discipline. Consider the debates, and changes of mind, in recent years on the issue whether homosexuality is or is not a mental illness; consider the importance attached not so long ago to the category of the psychopath, and the scorn that is now poured on the concept by those most devoted to extending the role of the psychiatrist in the treatment of offenders.

What this shows, I believe, is not that psychiatrists are not men of science; but that in the case of psychiatry there is a more than usual difficulty in deciding when men of sciene are testifying within their science, and when they are going beyond it. The difficulty is, I believe, a matter of principle, and not something which can be avoided in the particular case by an alert judge. The difficulty of principle is that in psychiatry it is uniquely hard to draw a line between matters of fact and matters of value: matters of fact, on which expert information can be given, and matters of value where evidence may involve the tacit conveyance of a decision on principle and policy which it is not the province of the expert to make.

There are three ways in which experts may usurp the functions of others in the legal system. They can usurp the functions of the jury, by 'testifying to the naked conclusion', instead of providing information about the accused to assist the jury in making the ultimate judgement about guilt or innocence. In another way the juridical process is distorted if experts act like judges, tacitly imposing on the jury a meaning of their own for statutory terms such as 'responsibility'. Finally, experts can usurp the functions of the legislature, by testifying on the basis of convictions of general policy, e.g., that people who are sick in a certain way should not be sent to prison.

Let us illustrate these dangers by returning to the point from which we started, the insanity defence and the defence of diminished responsibility in murder in English law.

The basis of the insanity defence in England and in most of the United States is the M'Naghten Rules, though modifications to these Rules have been imposed in most jurisdictions. The M'Naghten Rules were laid down by judges in answer to the Lords in M'Naghten's case. According to the M'Naghten Rules, to establish the defence of insanity it must be established that the accused while performing the criminal act 'was labouring under such a defect of reason, from disease of the mind, as not to know the nature and quality of the act he was doing, or, if he did know it, that he did not know he was doing what was wrong'. It has often been objected to the Rules that they are stated in exclusively cognitive terms: they allow for defects of knowledge, but not for defects of the emotions or the will. Should a prisoner be held responsible, the Atkin Committee asked in 1923, if he commits an act under an irresistible impulse? The BMA suggested to the Royal Commission on Capital Punishment in 1953 that it should be a defence to a mentally diseased person that owing to a disorder of emotion he did not possess sufficient power to prevent himself from committing an act that he knew was wrong. But the Commission preferred to abolish any such test as the Rules and to leave it to the jury to determine whether the accused when he acted was mentally diseased 'to such a degree that he ought not to be held responsible'. The Commission gave no clear guidance as to the criteria it thought the jury should use to reach the decision; and the same vagueness is to be found in the Homicide Act 1957 which gave partial effect to its proposals. The new Act, without abolishing the M'Naghten Rules, introduced a defence of diminished responsibility which enabled an accused in a murder case to be convicted of the lesser crime of manslaughter if the jury find that he is 'suffering from such abnormality of mind . . . as substantially impaired his mental responsibility for his acts and omissions in doing or being a party to the killing'.

The term 'mental responsibility' is a curious one. Whether someone is to be held responsible for his acts seems to be either a legal question – is a man acting in such and such a way in such and such a mental condition guilty of a legal offence – or a moral question – should people who act thus in such and such mental conditions be convicted and sentenced by the laws. The word 'mental' seems to belong with 'capacity' or 'disorder' or 'disease', rather than with 'responsibility'. In practice 'mental responsibility' has come to mean something very close to 'a mental state such that psychiatrists believe he ought to be convicted'. Because the word 'mental' precedes 'responsibility' the matter seems to be one proper for the expert evidence of the the experts on mental health and disease: namely, the psychiatrists. Because the matter at issue is responsibility, i.e. whether the accused is to be regarded as suitable for conviction and punishment, the expert is being asked to testify, in a case where there is no dispute about the acts and omissions of the accused, whether in his opinion the accused should be convicted. The common law rule that an expert should not be allowed to testify on the ultimate issue, abolished for civil cases by the Civil Evidence Act 1972, is now eroded in criminal law too. The question whether an individual accused should be convicted should be a question, not for the psychiatrists, but for the jury; the question whether persons of a certain kind should be punished is a question not for the psychiatrists, but the legislature. But a psychiatrist who is asked to give expert evidence when a defence of diminished responsibility is led can hardly avoid giving his opinion on these two matters.

If a psychiatrist is asked to testify whether the accused acted under an irresistible impulse, he is not in the same way being asked to give an opinion on the ultimate issue or on a matter of public policy. But he may in fact respond by giving such an answer, since the actual question he is being asked is an unanswerable one. It has often been observed that the step from saying 'he did not resist his impulse' to 'he could not resist his impulse' is one whose necessity is never scientifically demonstrable;[19] so too the step from 'he did not conform his conduct to the law' to 'he lacked substantial capacity to conform his conduct to the law' (the formulation of the American model penal code). The Butler Committee observed pertinently that in most cases in practice 'it is fair to say that the only evidence of incapacity to conform with the law is the act itself'.[20]

Since the occurrence of an irresistible impulse is generally admitted to be something which cannot be established by science, it is clearly not something on which expert testimony can speak with authority. But I would go further: the difficulty in telling the difference between unresisted and irresistible impulses is not a temporary and contingent one which progress in science may remove. The notion of irresistible impulse is an incoherent piece of nonsense.

If someone succumbs to the temptation of committing a criminal act there is no way even in principle of deciding whether he is a man of normal strength of will giving way to abnormally strong impulses, or a man of abnormal weakness of will yielding to impulses no stronger than normal. Shall we look at what he has done on other occasions, to throw light on his present state? But his behaviour at other times is equally ambiguous, as evidence. Suppose he has often previously acted criminally: are we to take this as evidence of chronically imperious impulses, or of chronic unwillingness to control himself? Has he lived a life of unblemished rectitude? Shall we say that this proves his impulses are no stronger than normal; or shall we say that the fact that he acted so out of character shows that this impulse must have been abnormally urgent, to have overcome the resistance of a man of such established self-control? Where the same behavioural evidence can be offered with equal justice as evidence for contrary mental phenomena, we can be sure that the alleged mental phenomena are metaphysical fictions.

We think that we can understand what an 'irresistible impulse' is because we all have impulses, and we know that they can sometimes be hard to resist. But if somebody acts on an impulse,

[19] E.g. *R.* v. *Byrne* [1960] 2 QB 396, 404, *per* Lord Parker CJ.
[20] *Report of the Committee on Mentally Abnormal Offenders*, Cmnd 6244 (1975) Ch. 18.

his action must be a voluntary action; and if an action is to be voluntary, it must be possible for the agent to act otherwise. The notion of irresistible impulse is an incoherent one; we only think we can imagine it, because we equivocate on the sense of 'impulse'. If 'impulse' means desire, then it cannot be irrestitible; but 'impulse' also has the sense of a mechanical force, which can of course be something which necessitates. Because we are constantly tempted to think of the mind as a field of ghostly paramechanical forces, we think we can make room for this misbegotten concept. It is one of the benefits which philosophy can confer in this area that it may cure one of the temptation to think of the mind as a ghostly mechanism.

Incoherent though it is, the notion of irresistible impulse seems at present to be a part of our ciminal law, since the decision of the Court of Appeal in *Byrne* that inability to exercise will-power to control physical acts due to abnormality of mind is sufficient to entitle the accused to the defence of diminished responsibility. Until it is overruled or altered by statute, there will no doubt be psychiatrists called by the defence to testify that the accused acted on an irresistible impulse. The only remedy for this state of affairs will presumably be for the prosecution to call a philosopher to testify that there cannot be any such thing as an irresistible impulse, and therefore the accused cannot have acted on one, any more than he can have murdered a married bachelor or stolen a square circle. The desperate nature of this proposal will, I hope, bring home vividly the indefensibility of the present state of the law.

There is indeed general agreement about the urgent need for reform, and many proposals for reform were formulated in the report of the Butler Committee on mentally abnormal offenders in 1975. Some of the recommendations of the Butler Committee were enacted in the Mental Health (Amendment) Act 1982, but none which concern the particular difficulties so far mentioned, with are treated in the Committee's report in the chapter on the special verdict.

If the Butler Committee's proposals were accepted, the psychiatrist would no longer have to testify on the question whether the accused was responsible or not, nor whether he had been assailed by irresistible impulses. Nor would he even have to say whether the accused's unlawful act was the produce of mental disease or defect. The Butler Committee considered this fomula (the Durham formula) for defining the cases where mental disease or defect should exempt from criminal responsibility, or diminish responsibility; but it rejected it on the grounds that it was difficult to be certain how much of a person's behaviour is affectd by mental disorders that he may suffer. Instead, following the lead of the *Code Napoléon*, it suggested that severe mental disorder should free completely from criminal responsibility. Thus, when the jury believes that the accused, at the time of his alleged criminal act, was suffering from severe mental illness or severe subnormality, it should bring in a verdict of 'not guilty on evidence of mental disorder'. The role of the psychiatrists would thus be limited to saying whether, at the time of the act, the accused was or was not suffering from mental disorder. This, surely, is within the expert competence of psychiatrists if anything is; and the Committee provides a commendably specific list of the conditions to be fulfilled if something is to count as a 'severe mental illness'.

The Butler Committee's proposals seem to me ill-grounded and dangerous. The Committee was well aware of the radical nature of its suggestion. 'It is true,' they say, 'that it is theoretically possible for a person to be suffering from a severe mental disorder which has in a causal sense nothing to do with the act or omission for which he is punished; but in practice it is very difficult to imagine a case in which one could be sure of the absence of such a connection.' It it surely rash to proceed from the difficulty of being sure that there is no connection to establish a presumption that there is a connection; a presumption which, if their proposals were accepted, would be an irrebuttable one. In fact it is not at all difficult to discover whether there is a connection, in the relevant sense, between the criminal action and the mental disorder. The test is this: do any of the reasons for the performance of the action involve reference to the mental disorder? Why did the accused kill the deceased? If it was because he believed he had been commanded by God to do so, or because he believed she was a snake trying to throttle him, then there was a connection; if it was on the basis of a perfectly reasonable plan to inherit her money, or to be revenged on her infidelity, then there was not.

Let us suppose that an academic suffers from paranoid delusions that his colleagues are constantly plagiarising his work, and that they are denying him the promotion that is due to his talents (which in his own deluded opinion amount to genius). This will bring him within the Butler Committee's definition of a severely mentally disordered person. Let us suppose that while subject to these delusions he makes careful and efficient plans for the secret poisoning of his mother-in-law, so that he can enjoy the large fortune which he stands to inherit at her death. It does not seem obvious that his mental disorder should excuse him from criminal responsibility for a premeditated murder which has no connection with it, in the sense that the topics of his delusions form no part of his reasons for committing it. No doubt his mental disorder entitles him to sympathy; he would be equally entitled if he was blind or had lost the use of his legs; but that would not exempt him from criminal responsibility.

We can go further. Suppose there was a connection. Suppose that because of his delusions he murders not his mother-in-law but the head of the department who has refused to promote him to a readership. Why should he, even in that case, be exempt from criminal responsibility? Because even if his delusions were true, they would not justify him in killing the head of the department. Surely the correct formulation is to exempt from responsibility only those whose mental condition makes them believe that they are performing an action which, if their beliefs were true, would not be wrong. But this would take us back to something very close to the M'Naghten Rules.

The mental disorder may lead to mistaken beliefs about facts as that: this is not a human being I am strangling but a lemon I am squeezing; or: this person is trying to kill me. These beliefs, if true, would mean that the act was not murder; the presence of the first belief therefore negatives *mens rea*, the second gives justification. Equally, either of these beliefs would bring the accused under M'Naghten defence: he would not know the nature and quality of the act he was doing. On the other hand, if the belief was not about the nature of the act, but about the grounds for performing it, this too could exempt from responsibility if the belief, if true, would make the act no longer wrong: for instance, a belief that the act had been commanded by God or was the only way to avoid a nuclear holocaust. But a mere distorted set of values would not excuse under M'Naghten; nor should it in any rational jurisprudence.

I do not pretend that a return to M'Naghten will automatically make it easy to settle just how the insanity defence should apply. Take the case of *Hinckley*. He said, accurately, 'I was found not guilty by reason of insanity because I shot the President and three other people in order to impress a girl.' Does this mean that he simply had a wildly immoral set of values, preferring that his name should be brought to a girl's attention over the lives of four people? Or does it mean that he had a very improbable belief, namely the belief that shooting the President was a means which would lead to his achieving sexual success with Miss Foster? One would need to see a fuller account of the trial than I have been able to reach to settle this question, but however it is settled, it seems likely that he would have been found guilty in accordance with the rules. In any event, the use of the M'Naghten rules to establish *mens rea* does lead to the asking of the right questions, whether or not, in a case such as that of Sutcliffe, it necessarily leads to the right answer.

It is when psychiatrists are testifying not about the states of mind of the mentally ill, but of normal people, that the danger of their usurping the functions of the jury is at its greatest. This is something of which the courts are well aware. In *Transport Publishing Co. Pty Ltd* v. *The Literature Board of Review*[21] it was said 'ordinary human nature, that of people at large, is not a subject of proof by evidence, whether supposedly expert or not'. And in *R. v. Turner* Lawton LJ said 'jurors do not need psychiatrists to tell them how ordinary folk who are not suffering from any mental illness are likely to react to the stress and strains of life'.[22] Expert witness is not only superfluous in such cases, it may well be damaging; it may lead the jury to shut their eyes to what they know.

[21] (1955) 99 CLR 111, 119, *per* Dixon CJ, Kitto and Taylor JJ.
[22] [1975] QB 834, 841.

If on the proven facts a judge or jury can form their own conclusions without help then the opinion of an expert is unnecessary. In such a case if it is given dressed up in scientific jargon it may make judgment more difficult. The fact that an expert witness has impressive scientific qualifications does not by that fact alone make his opinion on matters of human nature and behaviour within the limits of normality any more helpful than that of the jurors themselves; but there is a danger that they may think it does.[23]

For this reason, the courts have been particularly loath to admit the evidence of expert witnesses on the question of the veracity of the accused. The Australian case of *Lowery* v. *The Queen*[24] was thought by some to have set a precedent in favour of this; but the precedent was very quickly limited in the Court of Appeal in the case of *Turner* just cited:

'We do not consider,' said Lawton L.J., 'that it is an authority for the proposition that in all cases psychologists and psychiatrists can be called to prove the probability of the accused's veracity. If any such rule was applied in our courts, trial by psychiatrists would be likely to take the place of trial by jury and magistrates. We do not find that prospect attractive and the law does not at present provide for it.'[25]

It is time for me to sum up what I see as undesirable in the present state of the law about expert evidence. First, as we have abundantly illustrated, it gives scope for the expert to usurp the role of judge, jury and Parliament. Secondly, it brings the professions of the experts into disrepute. The spectacle of experts testifying on opposite sides suggests, however unjustly, the possibility of venality on the part of the experts. A distinguished law professor at Stanford has said 'Psychiatric testimony is so unreliable and up for sale to the highest bidder that it is a national scandal.' Thirdly, the inappropriateness of the courtroom as a place for sorting out the difference between genuine and pseudo sciences means that pseudo-experts can impose on juries, while

---

[23] Ibid.
[24] [1974] AC 85.
[25] [1975] QB, p. 842.

genuine scientists can be made to look fools in cross-examination by smart barristers.

There are two fundamental things wrong with present practice. The first is that the adversary system does not fit well with the use of experts to assist the court. It leads to dangers that the experts will be more concerned to assist one or other party to win their case than to assist the court to arrive at the truth. Secondly, the present practice runs counter to the profound truth of moral philosophy which is that there are no experts on morality. Neither judges nor bishops nor doctors are such experts; it is because there is no expertise that we have juries. Juries are chosen precisely because they are not and know they are not experts; they are living witness to the fact that in matters of morality no man is in possession of information denied to others. I am not saying that one man's moral judgment is as good as another's; that would be folly. But what makes one man's judgment better than another is not that he possess information that the other lacks: it is not knowledge, but wisdom. And whether somebody possesses wisdom is something which calls for a tribunal higher than any human court can claim to be. All we do is to empanel 12 good men and true on the optimistic assumption that everyone has an equal *chance* of being wise.

I have taken a lot of space to say what is wrong with the present system; I propose to be very brief in saying how it should be put right. This is no accident, nor even the result of bad planning. A philosopher who makes detailed proposals for reform will only reveal his own ignorance of procedural matters. But I shall make three broad proposals and leave those with more knowledge of such matters than I to say how far and how best they can be put into practice.

To remedy the abuses in the giving of expert evidence we should:

1 change those statutes, such as the Homicide Act 1957 which virtually force expert witnesses to testify beyond their science and to usurp the functions of the jury;
2 remove from the courts the decision as to whether a nascent discipline is or is not a science capable of providing expert evidence. A register should be set up of such disciplines, and those claiming to have developed a new science should

seek admission to the register. The procedure for application should be somewhere between the way in which an
inventor applies for a patent, and the way in which a
university gets a royal charter. The essential thing is that
the matter should be decided not by a judge or barrister in
haste, but by experts in adjacent disciplines at leisure;

3 take the provision of expert evidence as far as possible out of
the adversarial context. There are already several contexts
in which the court, as opposed to the parties, can call for
psychiatric reports, in deciding fitness to plead, and in
deciding on sentencing. In the course of the trial too, it
should be the court and not the parties who call on the
expert.

The Rules of the Supreme Court, Ord. 40, already provide for the
appointment of a court expert on the application of either party on
any matter on which a question for an expert witness arises; but
this at present applies only to causes or matters which are to be
tried without a jury. This should be extended to all cases. Moreover
the court should be not only permitted, as now, but obliged to
appoint two or more experts on any matter for expertise. The
evidence should only be admissible if the two experts were in
substantial agreement; it should be presented to the court by one of
the experts who could then be cross-examined by either party. This
would remedy the evil of the disedifying court tournaments
between experts, and prevent an aura of expertise being given to
testimony which would be controverted within the expert's own
discipline.

   These proposals are the barest sketch of a remedy for the present
unsatisfactory position. I must leave it to others to decide whether
the practical difficulties in implementing them would bring new
abuses in their train. I hope merely to have convinced my hearers
that some such reform is urgently needed.

Part II

Philosophy and War

5

Counterforce and Countervalue
(1962)

In a sermon on Easter Sunday 1958 Cardinal Godfrey spoke as follows: 'Nobody can subscribe to the thesis that it would ever be lawful to use indiscriminate nuclear weapons on centres of population which are predominantly civilian.' Moral theologians in this country appear to be in general agreement with the principle thus stated by the Cardinal. In what follows I shall take its truth for granted.

There are many nuclear weapons of different size and capability. Two years ago the NATO powers already had 77 distinct missiles either in preparation or in use. The destructive capacities of these weapons ranged from the equivalent of ten tons of TNT to many times the size of the bomb used at Hiroshima. For all these weapons, even the largest, it is possible to conceive a legitimate use. Several Catholic writers have concluded without further ado that the manufacture and possession of all these weapons by the NATO powers is legitimate.

The conclusion is too rapidly reached. It is possible to conceive a legitimate use for anything whatsoever. Pornography may be used to light the fire. Hitler's gas-chambers might have been used as stables. These possibilities do not excuse those who publish pornography, nor those who built the gas-chambers. We cannot therefore proclaim as a general moral principle that it is legitimate to manufacture anything which can conceivably be lawfully used.

The legitimacy of the manufacture and possession of nuclear weapons depends upon the circumstances of their manufacture and the intentions of their possessors. It is therefore surprising that many Catholics who discuss nuclear weapons have little or nothing to say about these topics.

A recent writer in the Catholic press, for example, questioned about the lawfulness of the use of hydrogen bombs, said nothing about their use against cities. Instead, he discussed the use of them against a fleet at sea.

It may be interesting, and even instructive, to discuss hypothetical lawful uses for nuclear weapons. But the interest of such a question is largely academic. If we answer it wrongly, it does not seem likely to go too hard with us on that account on Judgement Day. But the question of the lawfulness of what is being planned in our name with weapons manufactured with our money by a government elected by our votes is not an academic question. It is a question which it matters greatly for every responsible citizen to answer rightly. There is no more important matter of public morality in our day.

It is therefore important to come to a correct moral judgement about the nuclear policy of our government and of the NATO alliance. For if that policy is immoral we, as citizens of a democracy, cannot be held free of guilt if we lend it our support or consent to it by our silence.

Reasons are sometimes put forward why priests should not express a moral judgement about nuclear policy. To do so, we are told, is to interfere in politics, which is outside the sphere of religion. But those who say this, rightly do not hesitate to preach and write against Communism, which is a political system. Injustice does not cease to be injustice, and murder does not cease to be murder, merely because it is championed by statesmen or canvassed by political parties. Public morality is as much within the sphere of religion as private morality.

Sometimes we are told that Catholics can make up their own minds on this topic without guidance from their pastors. It is hard to know what is meant by those who say this. If they mean that Catholics can make up their minds rightly, then they are mistaken; for Catholics on this matter come to opposite conclusions, which cannot all be right. If, on the other hand, they mean that Catholics will unaided come to some conclusion or other, true or false, then it appears that they do not think that it matters, on such a topic, to be right.

It is very much to be desired that the Church's condemnation of total war were much better known, both among non-Catholics and among Catholics themselves. It is widely believed in this country that the moral attitude of the Catholic Church to war does not differ from that of the average patriotic Englishman. Everyone knows that Catholics have odd views about contraception and therapeutic abortion; but about war we are regarded by the man in the street as being substantially sound. People sometimes hesitate to consult a Catholic gynaecologist, but nobody minds giving a Catholic soldier a commission.

This should not be so. Catholics, and others who believe in absolute divine laws, are divided from the rest of mankind on a fundamental moral issue. Most Englishmen today believe that the way to decide whether any particular action is good or bad is to ask whether it will do more good than harm. If so, it is a good action; if not, it is a bad action. Thus, if killing this foetus will save its mother, then it should be killed; for the mother's death will cause more suffering than the child's. Thus, if contraception does no harm and prevents overpopulation, contraception is to be recommended. Thus, if the bombing of Hiroshima saved more lives than it destroyed, it was a good and praiseworthy action.

Those who, like Catholics, accept an absolute divine law judge morality quite differently. For them, the first question to be asked of any proposed action is: does it violate an absolute divine prohibition? Only if the answer to this question is no, can we go on to deliberate whether the action will do more good than harm. If the answer is yes, then the action is bad no matter how much good it may promise to effect, and no matter how much harm it may promise to avert.

One of the actions prohibited by divine law is the intentional killing of the innocent. Because of this, abortion is wrong no matter how therapeutic it may be. For the same reason, the killing of non-combatants at Hiroshima and Nagasaki was wrong, no matter how many good consequences may have resulted from it.

Catholics, then, must differ from most of their fellow-countrymen about the waging of war. Many people in England believe that there are some values which must be defended by all the means in our power. Mr Macmillan, for instance, has said: 'If we believe we should defend our civilization and way of life, then we should be prepared to defend it at whatever the cost.' Catholics must believe that there are no values which can be defended at the cost of intentionally killing non-combatants. This difference between Catholic teaching and the beliefs of our fellow-countrymen means that we cannot presume that the military policies of our government are such as Catholics can accept, just as we cannot assume that the state of English law about abortion corresponds to the law of God.

If our fellow-countrymen do not know that we differ from them about what is right and what is wrong in war we have only ourselves to blame. In the last war the obliteration bombing of German cities drew no concerted protest from Catholics in this country. Catholics today join in the national adulation of Churchill, who was ultimately responsible for that bombing.

On the Continent Catholic leaders have sometimes been more outspoken. In 1950 the Cardinals and Archbishops of France wrote as follows:

> The question is persistently put to you, to your priests and bishops, asking whether we condone the use of these atomic weapons. But such a question, addressed to the disciples of Christ, scandalizes and revolts them. As the Pope said two years ago, no one 'with a true sense of humanity' can approve the use of modern weapons which strike indiscriminately at soldiers and civilians, and which blindly spread death over areas which daily grow wider and wider with man's increasing scientific knowledge. For our part we condemn them with all our strength, as we had no hesitation in condemning the mass bombing during the last war which, in attacks on military objectives, killed old men, women and children at the same time.

Since the French hierarchy wrote these words, it can hardly be said that Catholic statesmen on the Continent have acted in accordance with them.

When we attempt to come to a decision about the morality of Western policies of nuclear deterrence, we must not begin by asking whether these policies do more good or harm. We must first ask whether they violate the divine command against killing the innocent. It may be that the consequences of nuclear disarmament will be very terrible. None the less, we must disarm if the retention of nuclear weapons turns out to be immoral.

Since the use of large-scale nuclear weapons on cities is unlawful, it is clear that a government which possess such weapons as a deterrent can be justified, if at all, only if it does not intend ever to use them on civilian targets. It follows also that a citizen can support a deterrent policy only if he has good reason to believe that his government has no intention of using its deterrent weapons in murderous fashion.

Is this the case in the West today?

We must first notice that Western governments have in the past explicitly threatened to use nuclear weapons in an unlawful manner. The British White Paper on Defence in 1958 spoke of 'the balancing fears of mutual annihilation' and went on to say:

> It must be well understood that, if Russia were to launch a major attack on them [the NATO powers], even with conventional forces only, they would have to hit back with strategic weapons. In fact, the strategy of NATO is based on the frank recognition that a full-scale Soviet attack could not be repelled without resort to a massive nuclear bombardment of the sources of power in Russia.

President Eisenhower, in his State of the Union Message of the same year, had this to say:

> The most powerful deterrent to war lies in the retaliatory power of our Strategic Air Command and the aircraft of our navy. They present to any potential attacker the prospect of virtual annihilation of his own country. Even if we assume a surprise attack on our own bases, our bombers would immediately be on their way in sufficient strength to accomplish this mission of retaliation.

It is quite clear that the execution of this threat of annihilation would be a crime of mass murder. However, since 1958 British Defence Ministers have come and gone, and the Eisenhower administration has been replaced by that of President Kennedy. No more has been heard of the threat to reply to a conventional Russian attack with a nuclear bombardment. But in 1962 as in 1958 the threat of massive retaliation remains.

At a meeting of NATO ministers in Athens in 1962, the Lord Privy Seal reported, 'the council reviewed the action which it would be necessary for member countries to take in various circumstances in which the alliance might be compelled to use nuclear weapons' (*The Times*, 25 May 1962). On his return from this meeting Mr Watkinson, the Minister of Defence, announced that 'Ministers were agreed on the circumstances in which nuclear weapons might have to be used in defence of the alliance.' The first priority of the British effort in NATO, he continued, was to be 'the maintenance of the strategic nuclear strike force' (*The Times*, 10 May 1962).

The distinction between strategic nuclear weapons (those which would be used in a 'massive bombardment of the sources of power') and tactical nuclear weapons (which would be used on local military targets) is not necessarily a distinction between weapons of different sizes. It is said that missiles of the size used against Hiroshima are now regarded as tactical by NATO commanders. As Mr Watkinson explained in the House of Commons later in May, this distinction between weapons is primarily a distinction between their targets (*The Times*, 17 May 1962).

On 16 June 1962 Mr Robert McNamara, the American Defence Secretary, made a speech in which he denounced independent national nuclear deterrents as 'dangerous, expensive, prone to obsolescence, and lacking in credibility as a deterrent'. Surprise nuclear attack, he said, was not a rational act; but nations did not always act rationally. The NATO allies must frame their strategy with the terrible contingency of nuclear war in mind (*Observer*, 17 June 1962).

In the course of the same speech, however, Mr McNamara announced that in the event of a major war American strategy would be aimed at the destruction of enemy military forces, not of the civilian population. This, he said, would 'give a possible opponent the strongest imaginable incentive to refrain from striking our own cities'.

The American Secretary of Defence thus gave official sanction to a distinction drawn by nuclear strategists between a 'counterforce strategy' aimed at knocking out the enemy's strategic forces, and a 'countervalue strategy' aimed at destroying his cities. Since this distinction resembles the distinction made by Catholic teaching between the lawful and unlawful use of bombs in war, it is worth looking more closely at Mr McNamara's strategy to see whether, unlike the policy of President Eisenhower, it is capable of moral justification.

On examination it appears that Mr McNamara by no means ruled out the eventual application of countervalue strategy. In the same speech he spoke of America's 'second strike capability' as a deterrent to enemy attack on American cities. It appears therefore that the restriction of American aim to military targets in the event of war would be only a temporary measure. The strength and nature of the NATO alliance, *The Times* reported him as saying, 'made it possible for the United States to retain, even the face of a massive attack, sufficient reserve power to destroy an enemy society if driven to it' (*The Times*, 18th June 1962). Thus the old threat remained, relegated only to second place.

Some days later the American Defence Department issued estimates of casualties likely to be caused in the West if both the Soviet Union and the United States adopted a counterforce strategy in the event of a nuclear war. The estimates were given in *The Times* as follows:

> According to these official estimates the casualties in the West would be 25 million dead, compared with 215 million if cities were bombarded. The estimates are divided as follows: In the event of a counterforce exchange, 10 million dead in the United States and 15 million in western Europe, including Britain; in a general bombardment, 100 million in the United States and 115 million in western Europe.

Other American strategists put the figures much higher. The nuclear expert Herman Kahn estimated that Western casualties might reach 125 million. *The Times* report continued:

> Mr Kahn believes that in the middle and late 1960s, when the Soviet Union had increased its nuclear force and American missiles had been dispersed throughout the country in hardened sites, these estimates might be multiplied by as much as five. In other words, without civil defence the counterforce strategy theoretically has a capability of overkill, and could destroy all life in western Europe, the United States, and presumably the Soviet Union. (*The Times*, 4 July 1962)

These figures shed a lurid light on what Mr McNamara meant by 'aiming at the destruction of military forces'. To claim that a counterforce strategy of this kind does not involve an attack on civilian populations is like claiming not to be responsible for the death of a friend if one shoots a bullet to kill a mosquito perched on his throat.

Even so, Mr McNamara's policy was insufficiently ruthless to win support in the United States or in this country. In America influential strategists dismissed the 'Spare-the-Cities' strategy as unworkable. The British Defence Minister is reported to have said that British nuclear targets were too close to civil centres for the theory to work (*The Times*, 3 July 1962). When Mr Thorneycroft visited Washington in September to survey nuclear strategy *The Times* reported: 'It is apparent that the British delegation think little of the McNamara proposal of a counterforce strategy' (*The Times*, 12 September 1962).

At the time of the Cuban Crisis in October nothing more was heard of the distinction between counterforce and countervalue. President Kennedy simply threatened full retaliation on Russia in the event of nuclear weapons being aimed at American soil from Cuba. At the time of going to press, therefore, the official NATO strategy includes provision, in certain circumstances, for the use of nuclear weapons 'to destroy an enemy society'.

Such a use of nuclear weapons cannot be justified. NATO defence policy, therefore, can be justified only on the plea that these threats are not seriously meant. For if they are seriously meant, then NATO defence policy involves a readiness to commit murder on a gigantic scale. The intention to do so is admittedly a conditional one. But one may not intend even conditionally to do what is forbidden absolutely.

There are some people who believe that our governments do not mean what they have said. In the event of war, these people believe, our governments will be deterred by considerations of morality or self-interest from using nuclear weapons against cities.

Such confidence seems unfounded. Our governments appear unlikely to be deterred by morality. The governments of this country and of the US used bombs murderously in the last war and those who authorized such murder are still held in honour among us. And if they believe, as many people profess to, that it is preferable to die than to be governed by Communists, then our governments are unlikely to be deterred by self-interest.

Many of the nuclear weapons which are possessed by the NATO powers are of such a kind that the only profitable use for them is against cities. Devices such as that tested by the US in 1958, which burned out the eyes of rabbits 350 miles away from the explosion, would be difficult to put to a non-murderous use in war. Missiles such as Polaris and Skybolt are too inaccurate to be used against a target smaller than a city. The same holds of any intercontinental ballistic missile (cf. *The Times*, 21 April 1963).

There are smaller nuclear weapons whose use, in the abstract, may be justified. But while the great powers retain their large-scale weapons the danger of using these smaller weapons is too great; for the use of even the smallest of them risks massive nuclear retaliation.

It is true that our governments hope that they will never have to use their nuclear weapons at all, and that their avowed purpose in possessing such weapons is to reduce the risk of war. None the less, they are prepared, if pushed to it, to wage thermonuclear war. At the time of the Cuban Crisis President Kennedy, backed by American public opinion, threatened the Russians with such war. Neither those who praised his action nor those who blamed it have suggested that he was merely bluffing: and Mr Khrushchev took the threat with full seriousness.

On reflection, it is obvious that if the use of large-scale nuclear weapons is immoral then their possession as a deterrent must be so also. If nuclear weapons could be maintained and operated by one man alone, then that man might possess them as a deterrent and keep to himself the fact that he intended never to use them. But nuclear weapons are not like a revolver that can be kept locked in drawer. The maintenance of the deterrent demands that the enemy shall believe that the deterring power is both able and willing to use the deterrent. But no democratic power can convince its enemies that it is able and willing to use its deterrent unless it has military units willing to operate the deterrent if ordered and parliamentary sanction to order its operation if necessary. Now what deters is not the threat of the lawful use of nuclear weapons, but the threat of their murderous use. If the Russians are deterred by the nuclear armoury of the West, it is not because they are afraid of field artillery such as Honest Johns: it is because they are afraid of the obliteration of their cities. The maintenance of the Western deterrent therefore demands that Western military men shall be ready to commit murder if ordered to do so, and that Western parliamentarians shall sanction the ordering of murder by government if government deems it necessary.

The conclusion seems unavoidable that no Catholic may play a part in the maintenance of the NATO deterrent, nor support any policy which involves this strategy. Nor is this all. We must not only not consent to murder, we are obliged to do all we reasonably can to prevent its commission. What are the best methods to achieve this, is another question. It is possible to admire the aims of the Committee of 100 without feeling that they have chosen wise methods of pursuing them. But the plans which are being made in our name are criminal on too vast a scale for us to rest content with a vague wish that things were not as they are.

Those who have followed my argument will see that I recommend nuclear disarmament not as a policy but as a moral imperative. We must give up our nuclear deterrent not because by so doing we shall achieve some desirable aim, but because to retain it is wicked. What will then follow is not in our hands. The prospect of standing defenceless before Communist Russia is indeed a sombre one. But that does not justify us in covenanting with the NATO powers to commit murder. *Neque ab Oriente, neque ab Occidente: Deus judex est.*

6

'Better Dead than Red'
(1984)

In the course of argument about the morality of nuclear weapons sooner or later the slogan 'Better dead than red' may be introduced. Possibly a defender of the use of these weapons may employ the phrase. Much more likely he may be accused by his opponent of maintaining a position which can be thus summed up. Sophisticated defenders of Western nuclear policy are likely to disown the slogan, but I think it is worth taking seriously because, in my view, it does contain a certain amount of truth. Like most slogans, it can be taken in many different senses. It is a help in clarifying one's thinking about nuclear war and nuclear deterrence to attempt to sort out in what sense the slogan is true or defensible.

'Better dead than red' may be an expression of preference or the expression of a moral judgement. Most likely it is the latter, but there are many different judgements which it may express. Perhaps it means that one should die rather than become a Communist; or that one should be prepared to kill and die rather than submit to Communist rule; or that it is better that there should be a large number of deaths in a nuclear war than that the West should be overcome by communism. Let us examine various possible meanings of the slogan in turn.

'Better dead than red' may be a dramatic expression of the moral judgement that one ought not to become a Communist. A religious person, believing that to embrace Communism is incompatible with his religious beliefs, might affirm that one should be martyred rather than become a Communist. Except on religious grounds it is hard to see how one could substantiate a totally general moral principle that it was wrong to join a Communist Party: there may well be stages in the history of particular societies in which membership of a Communist Party is preferable to any of the possible political alternatives, and where the injustice of the existing system is so palpable that political inactivity would involve complicity in tyranny. But the record of most Communist Parties which have come to power has been a record of ruthlessness and oppression; and I have no doubt that it would be a disaster for a country such as the UK or the USA to come under Communist rule. Hence I think it quite wrong to join an organization that has such a goal, and I hope I would not do so even to save my life. In that sense, I am willing to subscribe to the motto 'Better dead than red'.

But the slogan, in this sense, is irrelevant to the consideration of nuclear warfare and indeed to almost any real-life situation. Even the most rigidly organized socialist countries no one is faced with the choice between joining the Party and being put to death. Individuals are indeed forced to make choices between joining the Party and giving up all hope of power and influence; or between joining the Party and losing their friends, their career and perhaps their livelihood. In such circumstances to refuse to join the Party can and does call for heroism, and nobody who has not been faced with the choice can know whether he or she would display the necessary heroism. But 'Better live on bread and water than join the Party' is a moral principle which, however admirable, has clearly nothing to do with questions of the rights and wrongs of nuclear warfare and deterrence.

In fact 'Better dead than red' is more likely to express a principle not about preferring death to becoming a Communist, but about preferring death to coming under Communist rule. It may be a simple expression of preference: 'I would rather die than come under Communist rule.' As an expression of preference, it cannot be used directly to bring pressure to bear on others. It is more important to evaluate it as the expression, not of a preference, but of a moral principle: that one should prefer death to Communist domination.

This principle itself can be taken in several ways. Most plausibly, it means: one should die rather than submit to Communist rule. Someone might hold this in the extreme form of believing that one should kill oneself rather than fall into Communist power. I believe this is a mistaken moral judgement, but I would not wish to argue with people who hold it. They can, when the time comes, act upon their principle without involving us or anyone else in war, nuclear or otherwise, in the meantime.

It is more likely that someone would espouse the principle: one ought to be prepared to be killed rather than submit to Communist rule. This principle, indeed, I myself believe to be correct. That is to say, I think that a citizen of a country such as ours can and should be prepared to risk his life to prevent the country from being invaded by a Communist power or overrun by a Communist insurrection. In saying this, I realize, I am disagreeing with many of those in the nuclear disarmament movement. For many of those who oppose the retention and use of nuclear weapons do so because they are pacifists who oppose all forms of war. I am claiming that pacifists are wrong, and that there can be such a thing as a just war. Moreover, I am claiming that the independence of countries such as the USA and the UK, and the differences between the Communist system and the political system of our democracies are matters important enough to provide the grounds for a just war.

There can be, I claim, such a thing as a just war: or, more correctly, the making of war can be a just action; it can be morally permissible to go to war. The difference between the fomulations is meant to remind us that war is something which is brought about by human beings, is an activity which human beings engage in, and it is that which makes it a topic for moral evaluation. It is wrong to think of war as an impersonal event, something which happens or breaks out like an earthquake or an epidemic. It is not only wrong but dangerous, since it screens one's own and one's country's part in a war from moral scrutiny. A just war is not a war in which both sides are acting justly; on most traditional definitions of a just war that would not be possible, since it is a condition for a war to be just at all that it should be waged in order to right a wrong done, or to prevent an imminent wrong. There cannot be a war which is a just war in the sense that both the combatants are fully justified in fighting war; though, given the complicated nature of international relations, it may well be that both sides reasonably believe they have a just cause. But it can be just to make war in defence against those who are making war unjustly.

It is dangerous to think of war as an impersonal event: it is no less dangerous to think of it as a self-contained human activity like a game of baseball or cricket. To be justified, war must be an instrument of policy: it must be a means to a desirable, and morally defensible, goal. Victory is not in itself a goal which justifies war; to be able to justify a war one must be able to point to the goods to be achieved by victory. Winning a war is not like winning a game in which the aim is something which is simply defined by the internal structure of the activity. This means that the unconditional surrender of the enemy is not a legitimate objective of war, though one may rightly adopt a policy of unconditional refusal to treat with a particular government. Wars may be waged, not in order to destroy the enemy society, but to force the enemy to desist from the wrong in which he is engaged or about to engage. Spelling out the particular wrong which justifies one's taking up arms is *eo ipso* spelling out the conditions on which one ought to be ready to accept surrender (plus whatever extra conditions are necessary in order to ensure that the terms of surrender are observed).

Besides the necessity that a war should be waged in order to right a specific wrong, a number of conditions must be observed in its waging if it is to be morally justified. One is that the good to be obtained by the righting of the wrong must outweigh the harm which will be done by the choice of war as a means. Another is that the harm done in warmaking shall be no more than is necessary for the achieving of the legitimate goal of the war. A third, which only partially overlaps with the two previous conditions, is that 'the rules of war' (governing the treatment of combatants and non-combatants, etc.) should be observed.

The provisos which I have specified derive from the reflections of philosophers and theologians on the conditions for a just war, between the Middle Ages and the present century. The thinkers in question were mostly Christians, but there is nothing in their arguments which appeals to specially Christian premises; and several of the rules which they laid down have been embodied from time to time in international agreements. Nations vilify their enemies when they violate the rules of war, and proudly proclaim the fact when they themselves observe them. The rules are not a set of arbitrary prohibitions; they are an articulation of the only conditions under which the international community can rationally accept war, in the absence of an effective supranational coercive force, as a means of righting international wrongs. War is justifiable only if war can be limited, just as within an individual society, police forces are necessary but are tolerable only if there are limits on police powers.

The most important of the traditional conditions for a just war was that it should not involve the deliberate killing of noncombatants. This was sometimes called the prohibition on 'killing the innocent'; but the innocence in question had nothing to do with moral guiltlessness or lack of responsibility: the 'innocent' were those who were not *nocentes*, not engaged in harming your side. Soldiers who had surrendered were, in this sense, no less 'innocent' than infants in arms and had an equal right to be spared. The traditional principle is best formulated thus: it is lawful to kill only those who are engaged in waging war or in supplying those who are waging war with the means of doing so.

The principle, thus formulated, does justify the deliberate killing of more than those who are wearing uniform. It regards as justified, for instance, the killing of munitions workers, or of civilians driving trainloads or truckloads of soldiers. The unintended deaths of uninvolved civilians resulting from an attack on a military target (e.g. the blowing up of a castle, or the bombing of a naval dockyard) were likewise not condemned as murderous by this principle, which was concerned with deliberate killing; though of course they were something very relevant to the question whether the war was doing more harm than good. What was clearly ruled out by this principle was the deliberate massacre of civilian populations or the devastation of whole cities as an end in itself or a means to victory.

It is often said that the conditions for a just war were rules drawn up in a medieval context which are quite inapplicable in modern wars. It is certainly true that the rules are not often observed in contemporary wars; no more were they, for that matter, in the Middle Ages. But it is no objection to a moral principle to point out that people often break it; morals are about what we ought to do, not about what we in fact do. It would be as absurd to say that the rules of war are out of date because people nowadays do not keep them as to say that the law of contract is now superannuated because so many people go in for shoplifting.

But a distinction can no longer be made between combatants and non-combatants, we are told, because nowadays war is total and the whole community is involved in total war. If what is meant by saying that war is total is that nowadays war is waged *by* whole communities, then it is untrue that any war is total. Even at the point of maximum mobilization in the Second World War a large part of the population of the warring nations consisted of children or of those who were maintaining the services that would have been essential even if the nation had been at peace. If what is meant by saying that war is total is that nowadays war is waged *against* whole communities, this is unfortunately true. The relevant difference between us and medieval society is that we have become technologically so much more proficient at doing this.

But in fact the distinctions on which the rules of the just war were based were clearly applicable in the Second World War. The allies began the war with a cause which was clearly just: to right the wrong done to Poland and to prevent further aggression by an intrinsically evil political system. In the course of the war they violated the prohibition on mass killing on non-combatants not through any inability to notice a distinction between combatants and non-combatants but through a deliberate decision to ignore it. In the case of the UK the decision to change from a policy of bombing military targets to the policy of area bombing of centres of population was an explicit, and bitterly contested, decision at the highest level. In the case of the USA the decision to use the first atom bombs to wipe out the cities of Hiroshima and Nagasaki was taken – on the most charitable version of events – on the basis of a cool calculation that the devastation of these centres of population was the speediest way of ensuring a victorius end to the war.

Even in the nuclear age the distinction between a policy of attack on military targets and one of attacking centres of population is a very clear one. In the days when Mr McNamara was secretary of defence we were taught to distinguish between a counterforce nuclear strategy, aimed at knocking out the enemy's strategic forces, and a countervalue strategy, aimed at destroying his cities.

More recent US secretaries of defence have distinguished between 'soft targets' (the urban-industrial base of society) and 'hard targets' (missile silos and command/control facilities). So that even in the nuclear age the conditions for a just war are relevant; they are not antiquated in the way, say, that a rule that one should not take arms against one's feudal overlord would no longer have any application.

I have spent time sketching the just war tradition because I believe that it still provides the best theoretical framework within which to consider questions of right and wrong in warfare, and because it is important to show that the choice is not between espousing pacifism on the one hand and endorsing the nuclear strategy of the Western alliance on the other. Having argued that some wars *can* be just, I shall not spend time in defending the position which I have also maintained, that a (conventional) war to defend the UK and the USA from Communist domination *would* be just, provided that the rules of war were observed. There are, perhaps, few who would both accept the doctrine of the just war and deny that such a war fell within the bounds of a just war; but in any case the serious question is not whether a conventional war, but a nuclear war, would be justified in defence of the West against Communism.

It is in this sense that the slogan 'Better dead than red' encapsulates a certain type of defence of Western nuclear policy. The differences between the Communist system and our own are such, it is maintained, that to prevent the evil of having Communism imposed upon us we would be justified not only in going to war, but in waging a war which would violate the traditional rules for the conduct of wars: a war of mass destruction and indiscriminate killing. Better for everyone – both on our side and on theirs – to be dead than for us to be made red, than for us to have Communist rule forced on us.

I have been at pains to elucidate the senses of 'Better dead than red' in which it contains some truth because in this most important sense it enshrines a monstrous faleshood. No doubt a nuclear war could be waged in which only military targets were attacked: a war which ended after a first-strike exchange upon hardened silos in Montana and the Urals. If it was for this purpose that nuclear missiles were being stockpiled on both sides the arms race would be comparatively harmless and totally pointless; and the dictum 'Better dead than red' would be irrelevant to it. But the nuclear strategy which the stockpiles serve is one which involves as an option, at one or other stage, the use of weapons to destroy large centres of population, and to bring an enemy society to an end.

The exercise of this option is something which nothing could justify. The differences between the West and the Warsaw Pact nations are of two kinds, material and non-material. Western nations enjoy a number of material advantages by comparison with their Eastern counterparts: they can be summed up by saying that we have in general a far higher standard of living. More important, in the West we enjoy a large number of freedoms of which those living in the Soviet bloc are denied, and this facilitates the pursuit of many values which we cherish.

Nuclear attack on an enemy population is not justified by the defence of either of these advantages. Perhaps few would seriously maintain that one can justly inflict a horrible death on millions poorer than oneself in order to protect the differential between one's standards of living. But the defence of Western non-material values is equally impotent to provide a justification for nuclear massacre. Respect for innocent human life and for international law is no less a part than freedom of speech or rights against arbitrary arrest of what gives us a right to cherish and defend the values of Western democracy. To the extent to which we forfeit our respect for life and law we forfeit our claim to have any moral superiority to defend against Communist threat. As for democratic institutions, few of those are likely to survive a war in which both sides suffer nuclear devastation; to keep life going at all after such a catastrophe is likely to demand a social organization more ruthlessly authoritarian than anything now to be found on either side of the East–West divide. Even if the West by some miracle escaped devastation, so that the slaughter was one-sided, it would end the war having by its own act destroyed the claim that it possessed a system of human values which was worth defending; its institutions would deserve no more respect or loyalty than those of Hitler's Germany.

It would perhaps be very widely agreed – in the UK if not

everywhere in the USA – that the waging of nuclear war would be wicked folly. Even a Conservative government pamphlet setting out to defend the British independent deterrent begins by saying 'Talk of fighting a nuclear was is dangerous nonsense, because there can be no winners in such a conflict. It is no wonder, however, that there is a spate of books describing the horrors of nuclear war; for it is necessary to keep reminding people of what the world would be like after a nuclear war in order to bring home to them that there is no desirable goal which can be rationally pursued by launching such a war.

But while admitting that the actual waging of a nuclear war would be pointless as well as immoral, there are many who defend the manufacture and stockpiling of nuclear weapons as a deterrent. Thus the pamphlet already quoted says: 'the strategy of deterrence has held firm, despite the increasing international tensions of recent years, because it would be madness for either side to launch an attack on the other'.

If this is how the strategy of deterrence is enunciated, there seems a paradox at its core. If A tries to deter B from something by threatening to launch a nuclear attack on B, A is threatening to do something which on A's own account it would be madness for him to do. If B thinks that A means what he says, B must think that A is mad; if B thinks A does not mean what he says, then B must think that A is bluffing. Either way, then, B must think that A is either mad or lying: so how is A's threat supposed to provide a reason for B to act or to desist from action?

Perhaps when the Conservative government says that it would be madness for either side to launch an attack on the other, what it really means is that it would be madness to launch a first-strike attack on the other side, thus inviting nuclear retaliation. A second-strike attack, in retaliation upon a first-strike attack from the other side, is perhaps not, in the government's view, something to be regarded as madness; and it is *this* which provides the deterrent to a first-strike Soviet attack.

But would it, in fact, be a rational action for a country which had undergone a first-strike nuclear attack to launch a retaliatory nuclear attack? This seems to be quite widely assumed. Thus Senators Kennedy and Hatfield, in a book urging its readers to halt the arms race and support a nuclear freeze between the USA and the USSR, say: 'an all-out Soviet nuclear attack against the US would precipitate massive retaliation by American nuclear forces against the Soviet Union'.[1] The book questions many of the assumptions of current US and British defence policy, yet the authors enunciate this as if it was not in any way one of the assumptions which needs rethinking or questioning.

But would it, in fact, be the rational thing to launch a retaliatory strike if one had suffered the unimaginable horrors of a full-scale nuclear attack? A retaliatory strike could, of course, be viewed as an act of revenge; but few politicians, during peacetime planning at least, are willing to present revenge in and for itself as a respectable goal of policy. Otherwise than as an act of revenge, a retaliatory strike would seem to be at best pointless, and indeed against the striker's own interest considered from even the most strictly selfish point of view. A second strike would have no deterrent effect. It would by this time be too late for deterrence to have any force; it would not be like the punishing of criminals within a local society, too late indeed to prevent the crime which is being punished but calculated to teach a lesson to the individual criminal for the next time, and to all other citizens for the future. It would act against the interest of the striking nation; it would decrease the possibility of the survivors of the strike which has already been suffered receiving the medical assistance and economic aid which they will need if they are to rebuild anything of their stricken society.

The differences which at present exist between, say, the USA and the USSR would be insignificant in comparison with the differences between the USA as it now is and the USA as it would be after absorbing a full-scale nuclear attack, or the differences between the USSR as it now is and the USSR as it would be after such an attack. From the point of view of material civilization and technology, once the USA had suffered a nuclear attack, the nearest thing there would be to the original USA would be the as yet undestroyed industrial society of the USSR; it would be this hostile but kindred society which would provide the best hope, in the long run, of any eventual reconstruction of the USA along the

[1] E. Kennedy and M.O. Hatfield, *Freeze! How Can You Help Prevent Nuclear War?* (Bantam Books, 1982).

lines of the rehabilitation of Germany and Japan by the allied powers after the Second World War. From the non-material point of view, of course, the USA after having absorbed a nuclear attack from the USSR would have an enormous moral advantage over its enemy in that it was not – yet – guilty of mass murder on a scale unparalleled in history. But *that* advantage is precisely what it would throw away, in a matter of minutes, by launching a retaliatory attack. And it would be thrown away without the slightest prospective material advantage in return.

If both a first-strike and a second-strike use of nuclear weapons would be irrational, how can it be rational to possess them at all? How can it fail to be mad and wicked to threaten what it would be mad and wicked to do?

Thus runs a popular argument in favour of unilateral nuclear disarmament. The argument is powerful, but it is as it stands too simplified. It fails to take account of the fact that a power which has the capacity to retaliate with nuclear weapons is less likely to be attacked by another nuclear power than one which has no such capacity. The unilateralist needs to have a convincing answer to the question, frequently put by Lord Chalfont and others, 'Would the USA have used atomic weapons against Japan in 1945 if the Japanese had had the ability to retaliate in kind?'

The reason that the possession of nuclear weapons by *A* works as a deterrent on *B* is that *B does not know* whether or not *A* will be mad enough, when the time comes, to launch a nuclear counterattack. It is a nation's power, rather than its willingness, to use nuclear weapons, which is the essence of the deterrent. And however wicked it may be actually to use nuclear weapons against cities, however wrong it may be to be willing to do so, how can the mere possession of a power be something which is immoral in itself?

To answer this question, several points have to be borne in mind. First of all, if our enemies do not know whether we would retaliate by bombing their cities, neither do we. This is so whether 'we' means the electorate, the military command, the cabinet or the prime minister. Even the president of the USA does not know what any of his successors would actually do in the event of a Soviet attack on the USA; he does not know what orders he would himself give in any actual crisis. There exist, of course, many strategic plans worked out in detail; but which of them, if any, is ever put into execution no human being can foretell.

It is sometimes argued by moralists that a deterrent policy is a policy of bluff, and this must be wrong since bluff involves lying. This seems wrong. The deterrent policy would be one of bluff if our leaders knew that they would never give orders for a second strike. I wish it were a policy of bluff, but it is not: our leaders do not know what they would do, but they certainly do not rule out even in the privacy of their own minds the possibility of actually carrying out the threats which their policy involves. Lying is wrong, but the wrongness of lying is very much less than the wrongness of the intention to commit mass murder. That is why I wish that the deterrent policy were one of bluff.

But in any case, a deterrent policy need not involve any lying at all. Twenty years ago, in an excellent essay 'Morals and Nuclear War', the Revd Herbert McCabe OP wrote as follows:

> In order for [nuclear weapons] to be a deterrent you would have at least to pretend by lying that you would use them and lying – like the little girl in Rikkiti Tikkiti Tin – we know is a sin. This argument will not do because we do not in fact need to tell lies about our intentions. If I have rockets with nuclear warheads pointing at Moscow, however much I claim that my Christian morality would debar me from using them, Kruschev is going to be deterred from launching his. The Deterrent Theory therefore survives this criticism.[2]

The real reason why the maintenance of the power to destroy an enemy population is immoral is that in order for the nation to have the power, individuals in the nation must have the willingness to exercise the power. Everyone involved in the military chain of command from the top downwards must be prepared to give or execute the order to massacre millions of non-combatants if ever the government decides that that is what is to be done. It is true that this is a conditional willingness: it is a willingness to massacre if ordered to do so. It is true that it is accompanied, in every member of the armed forces I have ever spoken to, by a profound

---

[2] H. Mc Cabe OP, 'Morals and Nuclear War', *Blackfriars*, XLII (November, 1961).

hope that those orders will never be given. None the less, it is a willingness which is required and insisted upon in all the relevant military personnel.

This is what is really wrong with the deterrent strategy. To a pacifist, who thinks there should not be armies, navies, or air forces at all, it probably seems no great extra iniquity that the military should be trained in readiness to massacre. To someone like myself, who thinks that the military profession is in itself an honorable and indeed noble one, it is very horrible that we should be following a policy which makes it a mark of the good seviceman to be willing, in the appropriate circumstances, to commit murder on a gigantic scale.

As I have said, a policy of bluff would be preferable to a policy of deterrence which involves a serious intention to carry out a second-strike threat. But a policy of pure bluff is not really possible. The secret that there was no real intention to honour the second-strike threat could never be kept. It would have to be kept to very few indeed if the power to carry out the threat was to be maintained. It would have to be kept, not only from the enemy, but from the deterrer's own population and agents. It would, in particular, have to be guarded from every member of its armed forces. In any case, an administration which, *per impossibile,* kept secret its own firm intention never in any circumstances to use nuclear weapons would have to pass this information on eventually to the succeeding administration if the bluff was to be maintained; and it could not bind these successors to secrecy to ensure that the policy remained one of bluff rather than of solid intent.

Defenders of the deterrent will argue that the conditional willingness to engage in massacre which is an essential element of the policy is a slight and almost metaphysical evil to weigh in the balance against the good of preserving peace. The moral blemish which this may taint us with in the eyes of the fastidious is at best something to be put on the debit side, along with the financial cost of the weapons system, against the massive credit of maintaining our independence and our security from nuclear attack. Unilateral disarmament might perhaps make our hands a little cleaner and save us some disagreeable expense; but so far from reducing the risk of war it might actually bring it nearer.

A defender of the deterrent may well admit that all-out nuclear war is a greater evil than Communist domination: not all deterrent theorists believe that it is better to be dead than red in that sense. But though nuclear war is worse than Communist domination, it is argued, unilateral disarmament presents a much greater risk of Communist domination than the maintenance of deterrence does of nuclear war. Suppose, for the sake of argument, that nuclear war is ten times as bad as Communist domination; still, unilateral disarmament makes Communist domination virtually certain, while maintenance of the deterrent presents no more than a 1 per cent risk of war. Hence the deterrent policy is ten times as rational as unilateral disarmament.

Many arguments of this pattern have been presented: the mathematics naturally varies from this simple form, and the particular odds and valuations can be the topic of lengthy argument. But the most commonly heard arguments against unilateral disarmament take the form of an appeal to two kinds of risk: the risk of nuclear war, or the risk of Communist hegemony.

Talk of the risk of war involves the fallacy of considering war as a self-generating event like a storm. It takes more than one side to make a war; a nuclear war would have to be something we were a party to no less than our enemies. The risk of nuclear warfare is not something which can be assessed without reference to our own future policies and decisions. This may seem to be a quibble: maybe our enemies cannot go to war with us without our complicity, but they could certainly attack us without our leave, and from a selfish point of view it is the risk of nuclear attack which is to be feared, every bit as much as the risk of a two-sided nuclear war.

However, even the craziest enemy is unlikely to launch a nuclear attack for no reason. He is likely to do so either in retaliation, or to gain some military or political objective. We can avoid attack of the first kind by avoiding first-strike action of our own; we can avoid an attack of the second kind by conceding the political or military objective to the enemy before he attacks. (If he is so crazy that he will attack us for no reason whatever, then no policy we can adopt is likely to deter him either.)

The risk that we incur if we disarm is not a risk of nuclear war nor of nuclear attack; we abolish the first by disarming and we can avoid the second by surrender. If we disarm, what we bring closer is not war or nuclear catastrophe: it is the possibility of nuclear blackmail, of being forced to surrender by the mere threat of nuclear attack.

Nuclear blackmail is not at all an impossible policy for an enemy to adopt; it is not even necessarily an irrational one for a nuclear power to adopt against a non-nuclear power. It will be remembered that it was advocated by Bertrand Russell: before the USSR produced its first atom bomb Russell counselled that the West should take advantage of its atomic superiority by threatening to bomb the USSR if it would not agree to international arms control. His suggestion was not taken, even though the Western powers had just emerged from a war in which they had shown no lack of willingness to employ strategic bombing as a policy for victory. It is indeed striking that the two superpowers, since they have had nuclear weapons, have never explicitly resorted to nuclear blackmail against non-nuclear powers, even when they have been fighting, and even losing, conventional wars with them.

It is not easy to assess the degree of danger of nuclear blackmail to a country which lacks nuclear weapons. In so far as we encourage other nations to sign non-proliferation treaties, we regard it as a danger which countries other than ourselves should be prepared to face. The USA and the USSR each believe that the other aims at world domination. I doubt whether the USA does and I do not know that the USSR does; no doubt it would like every other nation to be ruled by a pro-Soviet government in the same way as the USA would like every other nation to be ruled by an anti-Communist government. It does not follow that the Soviet Union would be prepared to use nuclear blackmail to make every country into its puppet in the way that the Warsaw Pact countries are its puppets. But that is certainly a possibility which cannot be ruled out. Nobody really knows how much of present Soviet aggressiveness is due to a desire not to be in a position of disadvantage in comparison with a hostile nuclear superpower. It is romantic to believe that it would altogether disappear if the USA ceased to be a nuclear threat; but it is surely equally unrealistic to think that it would persist totally unaltered.

In the end there is no denying that total unilateral disarmament by the Western powers would leave them vulnerable to Soviet nuclear blackmail if the USSR retains its nuclear arsenal. This risk, I believe, is one which should be faced: it is a terrible risk but a risk less terrible than that of nuclear war. For our nations to be reduced to the status of Romania would be far less of a disaster than for all our cities to be reduced to the condition of Hiroshima and Nagasaki in 1945. The degree of risk of the two courses is not something that can be quantified in any scientific way. Whatever the Pentagon computers may simulate, what will eventually happen will depend on unpredictable human decisions on both sides. But one thing is clear: accepting the risk of nuclear blackmail does not involve giving a blank cheque to *our own* leaders to commit mass murder in the event of war.

Attempts to base nuclear strategy on the calculation of risk leave out of account the most important thing. This is the principle, basic to European morality for centuries since its enunciation in ancient Athens, that it is better to be wronged than to do wrong. That principle holds good even when the wrongs in question are, considered in isolation from the question of who perpetrates them, comparable in scale. But of course the wrong we would do, if we used nuclear weapons in a major war, would be incomparably greater than the wrong we would suffer if the worst came to the worst after nuclear disarmament.

I have considered various senses of the dictum 'Better dead than red' and have tried to draw various morals from what is true in that dictum. Of course, the slogan may be used not to express a moral judgement at all, but merely to give utterance to a personal preference. If someone tells me that he would prefer to be killed in a nuclear attack than to be subject to Soviet hegemony, who am I to disbelieve him? But such a preference, if it is seriously thought through, can hardly be very widely shared. The inhabitants of Warsaw already suffer what we would have to suffer if we surrendered to Soviet nuclear blackmail. Yet in the worst days of martial law, can anyone really believe that what the Polish dissidents would really have liked would be for the West to put them out of their agony by dropping a nuclear device with the centre of Warsaw as Ground Zero?

7

The Logic and Ethics of Nuclear Deterrence
(1984)

The 1981 statement on the defence estimates says that deterrence 'rests, like a chess master's strategy, on blocking off in advance a variety of possible moves in an opponent's mind'. If one understands this, we are told, one will see how shallow are many of the criticisms made of Western security policy. The analogy of the game of chess has clearly caught hold of the imagination of some of those at the Ministry: the leaflet widely distributed by the Ministry of Defence Public Relations Department is covered with pictures of chessmen interspersed between the paragraphs it reprints from the 1981 estimates.

The analogy deserves to be looked at closely, because I think it is true that Western strategists see their task as being to discover and maintain operational plans that will resemble a winning strategy in chess. But there is a point at which the analogy ceases to work; and the point of its failure reveals the weakness of the deterrent theory. In terms of the analogy, annihilation by nuclear weapons corresponds, obviously enough, to checkmate. Just as the chess master tries to block off possible moves of his opponent by adopting a position in which such moves will lead to the opponent being mated, so the nuclear strategist tries to block off possible options of an enemy by putting the enemy in a position where those options will lead to his nuclear annihilation. Thus far, the analogy holds. But there is this big difference between chess and nuclear warfare: in chess you can only mate once, and only one side can be checkmated, whereas in nuclear war there can be more than one completely devastating stroke, and both sides may be annihilated in the exchange.

It would, in chess, be enough to rule out a move if it could be shown to lead to being checkmated; because, once checkmated, there is nothing more that a player can do; and a player who, at a given move of the game, has it in his power to checkmate has, within the game, nothing to lose by checkmating. But it is not enough to rule out a strike by nuclear power A that it could be shown that it would lead to a retaliatory nuclear strike by power B; for power B, by carrying out that strike, would be risking a counter–retaliatory strike by A. We claim to be able to rule out of consideration, in the mind of Soviet planners, a conventional invasion of Western Europe, on the grounds that this will lead to a NATO first use of nuclear weapons. But do not whatever considerations rule out the conventional invasion in the Soviet planners minds equally argue for the ruling out of the first nuclear use in the minds of NATO planners? If they would be mad to trigger off our nuclear strike, would not we be equally mad to trigger off theirs? If it would be rational for them to desist from their conventional invasion because of fear of our nuclear first use, would it not be equally rational for us to desist from our first use because of fear of their nuclear retaliation? Thus the logic of deterrence seems self-defeating.

The logic only appears to work, perhaps, because those who believe in it either fail to take the game of threat and counterthreat beyond the first move, or because they think that rationality works in two different ways on the different sides of the iron curtain. If there is any difference, the Ministry of Defence is anxious to overcome it: 'planning deterrence means thinking through the possible reasoning of an adversary and the way in which alternative courses of action might appear to him in advance. It also means doing this in his terms, not in ours.' It is hard to see how someone who does this can reach the conclusion that there are circumstances in which it would not be rational for an adversary to attack us, for fear of our nuclear retaliation, but would be rational for us to retaliate on him, despite the fear of his nuclear counter-retaliation. At any point where we are deterring him, he must be deterring us from carrying out our deterrent threat.

If there is any difference between the rationality of a Soviet conventional attack under the threat of NATO first use, and the rationality of NATO first use under the threat of Soviet nuclear counterattack, the advantage is surely with the former. It seems marginally more likely that NATO would at the last minute draw back from its threatened first use after a Soviet invasion, than that the Soviets would fail to retaliate after an initial nuclear attack from the West. The extra odium which attaches to the initiation rather than the continuation of nuclear hostilities, and the enormous riskiness of the first crossing of the nuclear threshold, make the NATO threat less credible than the Soviet one, to the extent that either is credible at all as an expression of a rationally devised strategy. To the extent to which we may believe that the West is more likely than the East to be deterred from nuclear escalation by moral scruples, the effectiveness of our policy in blocking off options in Soviet perspective is further diminished.

It may be countered that I have only succeeded in arguing that the deterrent is self-defeating by committing an error parallel to that to which I am drawing attention: having complained that others have not thought past the first threat to counterthreat, I myself have ended the story with the counterthreat, and have not taken into account the counter-counterthreat, the NATO strategic deterrent, which will prevent the Russian counterthreat from being put into effect. Did not the whole doctrine of flexible response depend on there being a large number of steps up the escalatory ladder? At each point on this ladder, escalation can be undertaken by one side only under the threat of further escalation by the other. So NATO's first-use threat may after all be credible, because though it could be neutralized by a Russian threat to retaliate, that threat is itself rendered impotent because of our ability to retaliate upon the retaliator.

But why should we stop at move three, or four, or five? Should not we be held back from using our ability to counter-retaliate by the Russians' residual ability to strike back in retaliation upon the counter-retaliatior? It would only be when one side had exhausted its arsenal, so that the other could use its remaining missiles without fear of drawing a response in kind, that there would exist the conditions for a threat which was not rendered impotent by a counterthreat. But this fact can hardly be relied on by an alliance considering the first use of nuclear weapons; for neither side could be sure in advance of being the one which ended up with the last glorious remaining weapons; and both sides know in advance that before that final stage is reached more than enough warheads will have been exploded to destroy many times the civilizations and populations that each side claims to be defending.

To say that deterrence is based on muddled logic is not, however, to say that it does not work. After all we are each afraid, very much, of the other's deterrent, whether this is or is not a rational fear, whether this is a fear of a rational strategy, or a fear of an enemy's possible suicidal madness. What I want to argue is that even if deterrence does, in some mysterious and irrational way, work to instil fear, it is still immoral to rely on it for our defence, as the current strategy of the Western alliance is committed to doing.

From the moral point of view there are three things wrong with the current strategy of the Western alliance. There are three main ways in which it can be criticized on ethical grounds. It is wasteful, it is dangerous, and it is murderous. It is wasteful as the current arms race involves an extravagant build-up of armaments which can serve no military purpose. It is dangerous as it enhances the risk of confrontations likely to lead to an outbreak of nuclear war. It is murderous as it involves plans which call for the wiping out in certain circumstances of large centres of civilian population. Because it is wasteful, dangerous and murderous the current policy of NATO is morally unacceptable.

The three kinds of moral objection are not all of equal weight, and I have listed them in order of increasing importance. Current policy is extravagant, but large military budgets are not inherently evil, and the arms industry is a great provider of employment and a fertile soil for technological innovation. It is the pressure of other claims on the world's resources, when much of the human race goes in need, which makes the extravagance of the arms race an immoral, as well as an imprudent, use of economic power. Current policy is dangerous but in a world in which nuclear weapons have been invented and cannot be disinvented, no defence policy is going to be free from danger. The objection to current policies is that rather than limiting this danger, as their proponents claim, they actually increase it. This objection needs careful argument which takes account of the probabilities of different outcomes, and the magnitude of the catastrophes involved in each probable outcome. I shall try to present such an argument in another paper.[1] For the present I shall concentrate on the objection that Western policies are murderous: for this is the most fundamental and most serious of the objections.

Moreover, this is the issue on which a philosophical consideration of the ethical issues has most to contribute. In assessing whether a defence policy is criminally extravagant or unacceptably dangerous it is necessary to bring to bear technical information and to make necessarily conjectural estimates of the costs and consequences of alternatives. But though moral judgements can never be altogether separated from issues of fact, detailed factual information is less important when one is trying to settle whether current defence policies are murderous. When supporters and opponents of NATO nuclear policies argue whether they are or are not murderous, they are usually in agreement about the relevant facts, namely the nature of the proclaimed strategy. Their disagreement is a moral one about the wrongs and rights of the deliberate killing of civilian populations. What is most needed, in order to resolve this disagreement, is a clarification of the moral concepts and principles involved. So in what I have to say I shall concentrate on the issue of murder, both because it is the most important of the three moral issues raised by our policies, and because it is the issue where ethical clarification has most to offer.

My main concern will be to bring out what is wrong with current policies: I shall not be considering alternative policies. It is sometimes said, in criticism for instance of some members of CND, that it is wrong to condemn the nuclear deterrent if one has no alternative to put in its place. I do not think this is correct: one may be quite clear that something is the wrong answer to a problem without knowing what is the right one. If someone comes to me for advice and says 'Please tell me what I should do; my marriage is intolerable; the only thing I can do to bring this mess to an end is to kill my husband' I may perfectly well reply: I don't know what you *should* do, but I know you shouldn't do *that.*'

In this paper I am addressing myself to those who agree that nuclear war waged on populations or causing disproportionate

[1] See p. 108 below.

numbers of civilian deaths is morally unacceptable, but who accept with various qualifications the policy of possessing and deploying nuclear weapons as a deterrent.

Those who, while renouncing full-scale nuclear war, defend nuclear deterrence fall into two classes: there are those who justify possession of nuclear weapons as a deterrent on the grounds that some uses of those weapons may be legitimate; and there are those who defend the possession of nuclear weapons as a deterrent while agreeing that the use of them in all circumstances must be wrong.

It is possible to imagine uses for at least some nuclear weapons which would be legitimate. Considered in themselves, none of the traditional criteria for the conduct of just war would rule out the interception of ballistic missiles, the use of nuclear depth-charges on submarines, or the explosion of a nuclear weapon as a demonstration shot in an uninhabited area. In concrete circumstances, of course, such activities might be intolerably provocative or dangerous, and might well be intended as an expression of a resolve to proceed to more nefarious uses of nuclear weapons; but in the abstract they are morally defensible. But it would be folly to conclude that because some uses of some nuclear weapons are legitimate, that makes all possession of any nuclear weapons legitimate. The legitimacy of the possession of nuclear weapons depends on the purposes for which they are kept and the likely ways in which they would be used. The defenders of deterrence do not claim that deterrence can be maintained by the threat of these marginal uses alone.

The crucial question is this. Is there any use of nuclear weapons which is both ethically justified and sufficiently extensive to underpin the deterrent threat? Can a potential aggressor be deterred by a threat to do anything less than launch a murderous attack? Or must it be the case that any threat which is sufficient to act as a deterrent to our potential enemies is a threat whose execution would be immoral?

Before discussing this question we may begin by agreeing readily that the nuclear powers are in a position to inflict intolerable damage on an adversary without making use of all the capacity they possess: in order to deter they do not need to threaten to wage war to the limit of their strength. The superpowers could execute a deterrent threat with only a fraction of their present arsenals: this is one of the most frequent complaints of critics of the arms race. Even a minor nuclear power like the United Kingdom has the physical power to cause, with a single one of its Polaris submarines, damage on a scale which no Soviet government is likely to think tolerable.

But to say that the damage which a deterrent threatens is less than a deterrer, if unrestrained, could inflict does not settle the question whether such a threat of damage is justified. The Polaris warheads, for instance, in order to carry out a threat adequate to deter the Soviet Union would have to be targeted on cities or military targets in densely populated areas. The defenders of the deterrent whom I am addressing in this paper agree that the execution of such a threat could never be justified.

They argue, however, that a targeting strategy sufficient to deter need not involve any massive attacks on cities as such. An attack aimed at wrecking economic effort, transport systems and structures of command, in conjunction with a discriminating bombardment of forces in the field, could well cripple an aggressive regime in wartime and sap its will for military adventure while leaving the great majority of its population intact. Even such an attack would, beyond doubt, cause a large number of non-combatant deaths; but these deaths would neither be the purpose of the attack nor out of proportion to the presumed goal of warding off totalitarian conquest with the slavery and deaths which this would bring in its train. In absolute terms, the number of deaths could well be substantially less than the number thought tolerable in the war against Hitler.

Hence, it is argued, there could be a scale of strike large enough to rob an aggressor of the will to continue a war, and yet limited enough so that the expected harm to civilians is less than the evil expected if the aggression is successful. It is no doubt difficult to decide in advance, and in ignorance of the exact nature of the aggressor and scale of the aggression, the precise target-plan and mix of weapons of different yields required for such a judicious onslaught. But its possibility is sufficient to justify the maintenance of the deterrent capability to administer such a blow should the occasion arise.

Such an argument, in my view, is the most powerful form that an ethical defence of the deterrent can take. But though powerful, it turns out on examination to be quite inadequate for its purpose.

Whether an attack of the form described would be possible on Warsaw Pact targets in practice is something which is difficult to decide without knowing a considerable amount about the economic geography and military dispositions in the Soviet Union and its satellites. But we do know enough to show that no such attack on Great Britain would be possible. In Operation Square Leg, a government simulation of a Soviet attack on this country, no bombs were assumed to have fallen on inner London; it was assumed that five targets, such as Heathrow, were hit around the periphery. None the less the consequences, which are described in *London after the Bomb* (Oxford University Press, 1982) include five million dead in the London area within two months after the attack. Even allowing for the lesser density of the population in many parts of Eastern Europe, the result of an attack on military and economic targets in Warsaw pact countries is likely to be tens of millions dead. And of course many of the targets presented by the Warsaw Pact armed forces, on the hypothesis of an invasion of the West, are in friendly NATO nations.

But suppose even twenty million Russians, Poles, Czechs and their allies are killed in such an attack. Is that not better than that the West should succumb to totalitarian domination? Is it not a lesser number of deaths than were thought tolerable in the war against Hitler?

There is something grotesque in the idea that because the allies were justified in going to war against Hitler, then any war against a totalitarian enemy is justified if it causes less deaths than were lost in Hitler's war. First of all, the great majority of deaths in Hitler's war were caused not by the allies, but by Hitler's armies, Hitler's police and Hitler's gaolers: it is absurd to suggest that because we were justified in going to war against Hitler we would be justified in any future war in causing as many deaths as he did. Secondly, few would now claim that even all the deaths inflicted on the Allied side were justified: the lives lost in the bombing of Hamburg, Dresden, Hiroshima and Nagasaki by the Western allies, the lives taken by the vengeful Russian troops in their victorious advance to the West: these hardly provide a paradigm for the measurement of proportionality in future wars. Can we be certain that the war did more good than harm, in the sense that the world was a better place in 1946 than it was in 1938, or even than it would have been in 1946 had there been no war? Even if we can, that does not mean that we can lump together all the deaths caused in the war and say that the good it did was worth the loss of all those lives.

But even if we waive these difficulties, the comparison with the Second World War leaves out of account the most important thing: that the Third World War would be fought, as the Second was not, against an enemy who is himself armed with nuclear weapons. Even if a damage-plan could be devised which would satisfy the strictest scrutiny in accordance with the principles of non-combatant immunity and proportionality, putting it into action against an enemy prepared and willing to launch massive retaliation would be an act of reckless folly. The criteria for just warmaking include, it must be remembered, not only proportionality and non-combatant immunity, but also the hope of victory.

Defenders of the deterrent, faced with this objection, make two responses. First, they say that a victim of aggression cannot necessarily be held responsible for the response of the aggressor to the victim's self-defence: a woman has no absolute duty to submit to rape, for instance, even if she believes that resistance will lead to further violence. Hence, any Russian retaliation to a limited Western attack would be their responsibility and not ours. Secondly, we have no reason to assume that Western resistance on these lines would inevitably lead to an unlimited counterattack on our cities. In a nuclear war neither side would want escalation; both would be looking for ways to end the struggle; the Soviets would be no less anxious than the NATO allies not to put the cities of their homelands at further risk.

The first response commits an error opposite to that committed in the value judgement about the death-toll in the Second World War. It is a mistake to lump together all the deaths in a war and regard both sides as equally responsible for them: there is a difference between the lives a nation takes and the lives it loses. But it is an equally distorting error to suggest that a government can entirely escape responsibility for the loss of lives which it brings upon its own side by its attacks on an enemy. The major responsibility for such deaths does, of course, rest on the aggressor who causes them; but responsibility also rests on the side which, foreseeing the possibility of such retaliation, goes ahead with its own attack.

It is correct, as the second response reminds us, that there would be no certainty of a massive Soviet response to a limited Western attack: in matters involving human choices and decisions, in times of passion and confusion, there can be no scientific prediction or justified certainty in advance of the outcome. But in order for it to be rational to desist from a course of action, it is not necessary that it should be certain to have a catastrophic result; it is sufficient that catastrophe should be a consequence that is more or less likely. After all, the main reason for saying that it is not certain that the Soviets would opt for massive retaliation is that *they* would fear a Western response in kind. But that in turn is uncertain. The mere risk of such a response on our side is supposed to be sufficient to make them, as rational human beings, think twice about launching their attack; but should not the risk of their attack, at the earlier stage, provide an equally strong reason for refraining from the limited attack? Moreover, if the Soviets are deterred from a countercity counterattack, it is because they are afraid of an all-out assault on their population. But this, according to the defender of the deterrent, is something that would be immoral in itself, and the threat of which plays no part in the deterrent strategy.

It seems, then, impossible to defend the view that there can be a use of nuclear weapons sufficiently devastating to underpin the deterrent threat, while sufficiently discriminating to be capable of non-murderous execution. What of those who defend the deterrent while agreeing that no actual use of nuclear weapons is defensible? There are those who are resolved never actually to press the nuclear button, and who yet wish to retain nuclear weapons as a deterrent. This seems to be the policy recommended by the US Catholic bishops, and in the UK by Cardinal Hume: use is forbidden, deterrence is permissible.

The qualified approval given by these authorities to deterrence was no doubt influenced by the statement of Pope John Paul II to the UN special session in 1982. 'In current conditions, "deter-

rence" based on balance, certainly not as an end in itself, but as a
step on the way toward a progressive disarmament, may still be
judged morally acceptable.' The US bishops, in spite of their
profound scepticism about the moral acceptability of any use of
nuclear weapons, stopped short of an unequivocal condemnation of
deterrence, though they rejected any quest for nuclear superiority
or plans for prolonged periods of repeated nuclear strikes, and they
insisted that deterrence must be a step on the way to disarmament,
towards which they recommend a number of specific proposals.

Cardinal Hume, in an article in *The Times* on 17 November 1983
wrote that: 'The acceptance of deterrence on strict conditions and
as a temporary expedient leading to progressive disarmament is
emerging as the most widely accepted view of the Roman Catholic
Church.' It would be wrong , the Cardinal said, to apply to the
policy of deterrence the same moral condemnation that would be
given to the actual use of nuclear weapons against civilian targets,
which was something that nothing could ever justify. Since the
purpose of deterrence was to avoid war, servicemen could be
commended, and not blamed, for taking their part in maintaining
it. But the condition that deterrence should be a stage towards
disarmament was crucial: a government which failed to reduce its
weapons and limit their employment could expect its citizens to be
alienated from its defence policies. And finally deterrence had to be
seen as a means of preventing, not waging, war. 'If it fails and the
missiles are launched, then we shall have moved into a new
situation. And those concerned will have to bear a heavy responsibility.' How they should carry out this responsibility, the
Cardinal did not say; presumably, whatever they do, they must not
use nuclear weapons in the way he has already condemned, 'as
weapons of massive and indiscriminate slaughter'. The Cardinal
admits that his position is a strange one: 'There is a tension, then,
between the moral imperative not to use such inhuman weapons
and a policy of nuclear deterrence with its declared willingness to
use them if attacked. To condemn all use and yet to accept
deterrence places us in a seemingly contradictory position.'

Many, even among the Catholic Church, are yet to be convinced
that if all use is wrong, deterrence is still permissible. Some,

convinced of the wrongnes$ of the use of the weapons, deplore the lack of an authoritative and unequivocal condemnation of deterrence; others, accepting the Pope's judgement that deterrence, as things are, is tolerable, take issue with the US bishops' outspoken 'no' to nuclear warfare.

Is the position represented by Cardinal Hume in fact self-contradictory? Would a deterrent operated by people who believed that nuclear weapons must never be used be either credible or ethical? Would there be any point in retaining bombs that one was resolved never to drop and missiles one was determined never to launch?

It can, I think, be argued that such a policy is perfectly consistent with deterrent theory, as well as in accord with the demands of proportionality and non-combatant immunity. The point of deterrence is to provide an input to the practical reasoning of a potential adversary; if an adversary proves to be undeterred, then the deterrent has failed to be effective at the time when it was purported to be effective; it cannot, as it were, be made retrospectively effective by a retaliatory strike. The point of using it therefore disappears. Thus far, then, deterrence without use seems possible.

The difficulty in a deterrent policy of this sort is that if it is announced to the enemy in advance, it is not obvious that the possession of nuclear weapons would continue to deter. The proponents of deterrence normally regard it as essential that the possession of the weapons should be accompanied by the threat, explicit or implicit, to use them if need arise. Those who wish to defend deterrence while opposing use therefore have to be prepared to maintain that it can be legitimate to threaten what it would not be legitimate to do. Is this a defensible ethical position?

It may be argued that the threat to use nuclear weapons cannot be justified: for if it is insincere it involves deception, and it is not insincere it involves the intention to do what we have agreed it would be wrong to do. This argument moves a little too fast, and it is worthwhile taking it to pieces to see how far it works and how far it does not.

It must, I think, be conceded to defenders of the deterrence strategy that it is misleading for the arguments for and against the morality of the policy to be framed in terms of the intentions of the deterrer. It must be agreed that something less than an intention to use the weapons may be sufficient to deter a potential attacker. A mere willingness to use the weapons will suffice, a willingness which consists in preserving their use as a genuine option.

It is correct to make a distinction between intention and willingness: there can be a great difference between the two states of mind in degree of certainty and resolve implied. But making the distinction does not have a great effect on the course of the moral argument. If it is true that it is wrong to intend to do what it is wrong to do, it is equally true that it is wrong to be willing or ready to do what it is wrong to do. Any argument for the one proposition is an equally good argument for the other. If the wrong in question is an absolute wrong, then it is absolutely wrong to be ready to commit it, just as it is absolutely wrong to intend to commit it. To say that something is absolutely wrong is precisely to say that it is not a permissible option.

To reach a final assessment of the morality of the deterrent we have to ask: what exactly is it that does the deterring? As things are the deterrent has two elements. One is the physical element, the nuclear hardware and the power that gives to each side to destroy the other: this is what is sometimes called 'the existential deterrent'. The other is the political element, the declared intention or readiness of the two sides to use the hardware to destroy the enemy society in certain circumstances.

If our argument up to this point is correct, there is no doubt that the political element of the deterrent is immoral. But does this mean that one must unilaterally disarm? Not necessarily: that depends on whether the political and the physical element of the deterrent can be separated from each other. And whether this is possible depends on how the mechanism of deterrence operates.

The reason that the possession of nuclear weapons by *A* works as a deterrent on *B* has, in fact, very little to do with *A*'s stated policy. It is that *B does not know* whether or not *A* will launch a nuclear counterattack when the time comes. It is the nation's power, rather than its willingness, to use nuclear weapons, which is the essence of the deterrent.

Now if it could be severed from the *willingness* to destroy an enemy population, would the mere maintenance of the *power* to do so necessarily be wrong? That must depend, in part, on how the power is maintained. As things are, everyone involved in the military chain of command, from the top downwards, must be prepared to give or execute the order to massacre millions of non-combatants if ever the government decides that this is what is to be done. And this is one of the things most wrong with our deterrent strategy.

But must it necessarily be so, and is the only alternative total unilateral disarmament? Suppose that the Western powers announced a policy decision that nuclear weapons would never be used in an attack on soft targets, and that this decision was a serious and carefully though-out one. Suppose that all who were trained in the operation of nuclear weapons systems were given standing orders that it was strictly forbidden to take orders from anyone to employ them on soft or unknown targets. Would it not then be possible, without incurring the guilt of our present murderous policies, to retain sufficient nuclear hardware to enforce the best disarmament bargain that we can with the Warsaw Pact powers?

Objections to this will take the form that such a policy is impossible, or that it is immoral. It is surely not impossible. A number of former US Secretaries of State have suggested that the West should renounce the first use of nuclear weapons. Such a renunciation would be compatible with continuing to train servicemen in the use of nuclear weapons; no one has suggested otherwise. Equally it would be possible for the West to renounce a second strike, while continuing to maintain, as a bargaining counter, some of the existing systems. But if both first and second use were abandoned, as a matter of genuine policy and not just as a propaganda declaration, then there would be no motive for any further build up of nuclear arms, nor for the retention of present systems except for bargaining purposes.

Such a proposal would be quite different from the maintaining of a deterrent on the basis of bluff. I agree with those who say that you cannot maintain a deterrent by bluff: if bluff is to succeed then you must deceive the enemy; but you can only deceive the enemy by also deceiving those on your own side who maintain the deterrent; and if you do that it is highly likely that the bluff will turn into reality. What I am talking about is not bluff and involves no deception; you tell both the enemy and your own forces that you will never use the weapons, and you mean what you say.

But if theoretically possible, would such a policy avoid the moral objections? Surely there would be a risk that even if there is an official renunciation of the use of nuclear weapons this will be insincere; and that even if sincere it may be reversed by later governments. The risk is genuine; but it is only a risk that our governments will do secretly or later what they do now cheerfully and continuously. It is a risk which has to be weighed against other risks; it is not an intention to do something absolutely immoral. Thus it avoids the objection to the murderous aspect of our present policies: it preserves the physical elements of the deterrent, *ad interim* and as a bargaining counter, but without the adoption of plans for murder as official strategy, and without demanding readiness to massacre from servicemen involved in its maintenance.

It may seem absurd to concentrate so much attention on the present intentions, attitudes and options of those responsible for the operation of the deterrent. Surely there is a huge gap between mental states of this kind and actual deeds in warfare: is it not infantile idealism to insist so heavily on purity of intention in policy-makers and strategists? After all, even Christians do not seem to take very literally the saying of Jesus that he who lusts after another woman is an adulterer, or St John's teaching that he who hates his brother is a murder. Surely it is elsewhere that we should be looking for the morally relevant features of our nuclear policies: we should be weighing up the risks of deterrence against the risks of disarmament.

We shall come to weigh up the risks in a moment; but we must first insist that it is not, in this case, unpractical idealism to focus attention on the peacetime attitudes of those in power and those who serve in the armed forces. In an old-fashioned war there was much time for reflection, for changes of mind, for cabinet discussion, for weighing the pros and cons of strategies, for investigating and evaluating alternative options and battle plans. The actual decisions of the British War Cabinet in the Second World War were very different from anything that the members of the cabinet would have foreseen or planned before the war. (Not, of course, that the changes of mind were always an improvement from the ethical point of view!) But in the Third World War all will be different: the speed with which decisions will have to be taken will mean that the peacetime attitudes and planning of those involved will play the decisive role.

If a nuclear exchange should ever take place, then the key links in the causal chain which will have led up to it will be the options drawn up in peacetime, and the prewar intentions, attitudes and mental sets of those who take the eleventh-hour decisions which ignite the holocaust. This fact was well dramatized in a sequence in the film *The Day After*. The American personel who have, in a matter of moments, launched the intercontinental ballistic missile for which they are responsible discuss whether they are obliged to remain at their post by the empty silo. They are persuaded to go home and await there the incoming Soviet missiles. 'After all,' they say, 'the war is over now; we have done our duty.'

There will, however, one hopes, be a moment for change of heart or last-minute repentance on the part of those who now proclaim that if it comes to the clinch they will launch a nuclear attack rather than surrender. This, indeed, is the key issue at the heart of the ethical debate about deterrence: the question 'What do you do if the deterrent fails?' This is the question which Cardinal Hume declined to answer: but it is the one question which separates the sheep from the goats. In argument with defenders of the deterrent, there always comes a point where one wishes to put this question to one's interlocutor:

> Suppose that deterrence breaks down: suppose, that is, that you are faced with a choice of carrying out the deterrent threat, or of forfeiting the good things which the deterrent was meant to protect. What do you do then? I accept that the whole point of having a deterrent is to prevent being faced with the choice of using it or surrendering; but one can have no certainty that this choice will never have to be faced. Suppose that it fails, and you are faced with the choice: what, in your heart, do you think you should do?

If my friend says that if, God forbid, it ever did come to such a point, then obviously the only thing to do is to surrender – if he says that, then I know that fundamentally we are morally at one, and we can settle down in a comparatively relaxed way to discuss questions of risk and danger and expense. But if he says 'Well, I hate to have to say it, but if you are committed to the deterrent, you have to stick to what you believe in and you must go right on and use it if it ever comes to the crunch' – if he says that and means it, then I can only tell him, quite soberly and literally, that he is a man with murder in his heart.

8

Risk, Recklessness and Extravagance
(1984)

In the previous essay, I argued against the NATO deterrent policy on the grounds that it involved a readiness to commit deliberate murder. In this essay I want to explore the other objections to the policy which I summed up under the headings of danger and extravagance.

We have argued that any threat which was sufficient to act as a deterrent to our potential enemies would be a threat whose actual execution would be immoral. It is true that not every use, even of large-scale nuclear weapons, need involve deliberate attacks on cities. An attack on an army on the move in an unpopulated area, or on missile sites far away from civil habitation, would not necessarily violate the principles of just warmaking even if made with nuclear weapons.

But this is true only if we consider such attacks in the abstract. Neither large-scale attacks on military targets away from the front, nor attacks with small battlefield weapons on the central front, would serve any directly military purpose in the sense of bringing victory closer in the particular battle engaged. At most they would be an expression of political will which would act on the political will of the enemy. In so far as the political will which they expressed was the willingness to proceed up the ladder of escalation until the point of strategic exchange was reached, they would simply be a particularly clangorous expression of the state of mind which I have been arguing is immoral. But whether or not this is so, the firing of a 'warning shot' in this way is likely to be ineffective and extremely dangerous.

If the Russians have reached a point where they are willing to invade Western Europe, they must already have considered, and discounted, the NATO threat of first tactical use. They are unlikely, therefore, to stop in their tracks when that threat is carried out; and there is a likelihood that they will carry out their own declared threat of retaliating to NATO's tactical use with a massive attack on European if not American centres of strategic nuclear power; an attack which would be likely to carry with it the destruction of much of Britain. And if the carrying out of the threat would be enormously dangerous, the actual making of the threat can hardly carry credibility. The need to get the unanimous agreement of at least the major NATO powers makes it unlikely that the threat would be carried out, or at least carried out in time to stem the conventional defeat which it is intended to avert.

But let us waive these difficulties and suppose, as the Ministry of Defence invites us to do, that a war can be waged in Europe, using nuclear weapons, which can be brought to a successful end without leading to a strategic exchange (in the sense that no warheads fall on US or USSR soil) or involving deliberate attacks on cities taking populations as targets. Would such a war be a morally acceptable option?

Let us remember that in civil life a killer can be convicted of murder even though he did not intend to kill his victim; even though the victim's death was neither a means nor an end which he had chosen in carrying out his purposes. A death which is foreseen but not intended can amount to murder if the killer's action demonstrates, in the words of the American model penal code, a reckless disregard of human life. Not every action which results in a foreseen but unintended death is murderous; but the failure to take precautions, when engaging in dangerous conduct, or the triviality of the goal pursued to which death is seen as a possible by-effect, may manifest the disregard of human life which turns reckless killing into murder.

Similarly, in wartime, it would not be sufficient to rebut a charge that one's use of weapons was murderous if one could show that the weapons were aimed at, and had the sole purpose of, destroying a military target. For the weapons might unintentionally cause a number of civilian casualties wholly out of proportion to the military goal to be achieved. That is why, among the rules for the just war which govern *ius in bello* there is a condition of proportionality along with the condition of non-combatant immunity.

Both in peace and war murder can be committed not only intentionally, but also recklessly; not only when civilian deaths are the purpose of the strike as in terrorist bombing, but when they are the unintended result of the strike, as might be if a one-megaton bomb was dropped on Moscow to wipe out a command and control centre there.

Not every unintended death of a civilian following an attack on a military target counts as murder; an attack on a barracks may be justified even if it leads to the death of the cleaners and canteen workers. In the case of reckless killing, as opposed to intentional killing, there is room for the weighing of the costs and benefits. That is why the principle here is one of proportionality. But disproportionate civilian casualties can make an attack on a military target as murderous as an attack on a city.

Lord Zuckerman, the former Chief Government Scientific Adviser, is quoted in *The Church and the Bomb* (Hodder and Stoughton, 1982) as saying 'It is still inevitable that were military installations rather than cities to become the objective of nuclear attack, millions, even tens of millions, of civilians would be killed, whatever the proportion of missile sites, airfields, armament plants, ports and so on that would be destroyed.' If this is so, then it seems that an attack of this kind on military targets in the central European theatre would count as reckless murder.

Now, of course, it is possible to imagine military uses of nuclear weapons on a much less devastating scale. A Lance missile has a range of 75 miles with an average accuracy to within 50 yards, and its yield is a mere 10 kilotons; the use of one of these on a massive tank formation at the rear of attacking Warsaw Pact forces might be argued, considered in itself, to be within the bounds of proportionate military force. To use more than a fraction of the 500 stockpiled would quickly take us beyond the bounds, no doubt; but that is not the most serious objection to even the limited nuclear strike which would be represented by the use of Lances alone. If Lances were all that NATO had by way of nuclear weapons, then the use of them could be judged on their own merits. But the use of them is quite different when it is a step on an escalatory ladder. The use of Lances against the background threat of Pershing, Poseidon and Minuteman is a very different matter. In the familiar

metaphor, the use even of a single Lance would involve crossing the
firebreak between nuclear and non-nuclear weapons; and the
danger of crossing a firebreak depends on how great the fire-risk is
on the opposite side of the divide.

In present circumstances, any crossing of the firebreak amounts
to an unacceptable risk. This has never been put more authoritat-
ively than in a famous article by Bundy, Kennan, McNamara and
Smith.

> No one has ever succeeded in advancing any persuasive reason to
> believe that any use of nuclear weapons, even on the smallest scale,
> could reliably be excepted to remain limited. Every serious analysis
> and every military exercise for over twenty-five years has demons-
> trated that even the most restrained battlefield use would be
> enormously destructive to civilian life and property . . . The one
> clearly definable firebreak against the world-wide disaster of general
> nuclear war is the one that stands between all other kinds of conflict
> and any use whatsoever of nuclear weapons. To keep that firebreak
> wide and strong is in the deepest interest of all mankind.[1]

In the face of such warnings, repeated by many senior civil and
military figures who have been closely involved with nuclear
policies, an order to use nuclear weapons in wartime would incur
the guilt of reckless murder for all the deaths which followed from it
among the civilian population.

So far I have been presenting the case, based on risk, against the
actual use of nuclear weapons. I turn now to the risks of deterrence,
as opposed to the risk of actual use.

In order to weigh up the dangers of deterrence and disarmament
it is important to separate out in detail the risks which are run by
both courses. The risks on both sides can be classed in five groups:
the risks which concern our own future actions, those which
concern Russian nuclear attack, those which concern nuclear
strikes by third parties, those which concern conventional attack,
and those which can be summed up under the heading of nuclear
blackmail.

A nation which possess nuclear weapons, or even simply the

---

[1] 'Nuclear Weapons and the Atlantic Alliance', *Foreign Affairs*, Spring 1982, p. 763.

know-how to produce them, is running a risk that its own leaders, in the event of crisis, will use them in a murderous way. This is so whether or not the nation declares its unwillingness to use nuclear weapons first, or to use them at all on cities; it is so even if a nation actually disarms. But the risk is obviously diminished to the extent that the strategic policy is made less immediately dependent on the more murderous options. In one way this is the most important risk which supporters of disarmament seek to lessen; but of course in another way there is something rather odd in talking about it as a risk at all. Talking of what we, or those acting in our name, might do in a crisis as a 'risk' smacks of trying to distance oneself from one's own responsibilities. Taking risks about one's own future actions is not in the same category as taking risks about what might happen by natural causes or third parties or acts of God; and to treat it as if it were a form of bad faith, explored in detail by writers such as Sartre. If someone, anxious to put an end to an affair which is threatening to wreck a marriage, goes to a party where he will meet the beloved he is trying to give up, we regard his action not just as imprudent, but as calling in question the sincerity of his resolve to save his marriage. The matter is not quite the same in the case of national decisions, since the administration which presses the button may be a different one from the one that set up the button to press; but that is something that each responsible administration must have in mind, and each administration, in a democracy, acts in the name of us, the citizenry.

Opinions differ sharply on the question whether disarmament by the West will make a Russian nuclear attack more or less likely. On the one side it is argued that the removal of nuclear bases from Western countries will remove the prime targets of Soviet attack. Churchill, with characteristic pungency, said of the first American nuclear base in this country: 'We must not forget that by creating the American atomic base in East Anglia, we have made ourselves the target and perhaps the bull's eye of a Soviet attack.' On the other hand, it has often been pointed out that it is hard to believe that the Americans would have dropped atomic bombs on Japan if the Japanese had themselves had a nuclear capacity. Which side of the argument is right?

The answer lies, as so often, in making a distinction. The

removal of nuclear weapons surely makes a peacetime attack less likely. The only credible scenario in which the Soviet Union would make a peacetime attack with nuclear weapons on a Western nation would be in order, by a pre-emptive strike, to destroy that nation's own capability of launching a nuclear attack. If the nation voluntarily foregoes that capability, it removes the incentive for the Soviet nuclear strike.

Once a war has started between a nuclear and a non-nuclear power, the matter is altered. If a conventional war is going badly for the nuclear power, it may be tempted to use its nuclear power to right the balance (though fortunately the United States resisted this temptation in Korea and Vietnam). Even if things are going well, it may decide, as the United States did in 1945, that nuclear attacks are an acceptable way of shortening the road to complete victory. But the lesson of Hiroshima and Nagasaki is not that a non-nuclear power is always in greater danger than a nuclear power of being subject to nuclear attack. On the contrary, it was because Germany was believed to be on the threshold of becoming a nuclear power that nuclear weapons were developed by the US in the first place; and an administration more circumspect than Truman's, which might have had qualms about devastating the cities of an empire that was on the verge of surrender, might have used the first two atom bombs without compunction on nuclear installations in Japan had there been any. Again, had the Japanese been willing to surrender unconditionally in August 1945, as they were ready to surrender conditionally, the atom bomb would not have been dropped. Tragically, and senselessly, it was dropped and then conditional surrender was accepted.

I believe that nuclear disarmament would still, on balance, make it more likely that a country which was at war with a still armed Soviet Union would be subjected to nuclear attack. I conclude that it would be most unwise for a country thus disarmed to get involved in a war with the Soviet Union. But I do not regard this as a strong argument against disarmament. It is not as if we were now in a position where we could go to war with the Soviet Union with our heads held high and a song in our hearts; by nuclear disarmament we would not be giving up an option which we now have of taking the Russians on in a war it would be rational to wage. Just causes for war against the Soviet Union there have been in plenty; but of the other conditions of just war at least one has been missing since 1949: the hope of victory.

Even if disarmament reduces the risk of nuclear devastation by Soviet attack, we are often reminded there will always remain the possibility of a nuclear war between third parties. Whether or not this involves ourselves indirectly, it is something which we have a duty to prevent as far as we can; hence, if keeping our deterrent will help prevent such war, we have a duty to keep it.

Those who argue in this way have to view nuclear weapons in our hands as being fundamentally different from the same weapons in anyone else's hands. We encourage other nations to sign non-proliferation treaties, on the grounds that the more countries who possess nuclear weapons the greater the risk of war. But by a unique favour of providence our own nuclear weapons have the exactly opposite quality that, alone among the weapons systems of the world, they actually decrease the risk of war. Whatever the risks of being a non-nuclear power in a world of nuclear superpowers, they are risks which we constantly exhort every other nation to take. How can we consistently refuse to run them ourselves?

You may be surprised to see that I have not listed, among the risks on each side, the risk of nuclear war by accident. That is because I do not think that there is, strictly speaking, any such risk. There is a risk, and a horrible one, of a nuclear explosion by accident; the explosion of a warhead by machine failure involving no human decision. There is also a risk that, due to the malfunction of information-gathering or processing systems, decision-makers in the governments of nuclear powers may be led to make decisions of life and death on the basis of faulty data. But nuclear war cannot be launched except by the decisions of human beings, whether in the West or in the East or among third parties. That is why the risk of nuclear war by accident is really reducible to the three kinds of risk we have been talking about.

I turn to the fourth kind of risk: the risk of conventional war, or, more precisely, the risk of a conventional attack upon us by an enemy; because I presume we do not wish to retain the option of ourselves making a conventional aggressive attack. This is a genuine risk, and one which is increased by nuclear disarmament if that is a step taken without a strengthening of conventional defences. But I believe that the risk can be diminished by strengthening our conventional forces, and strengthening them in a way which can be clearly seen to be non-provocative and purely defensive. And I believe further that recent developments in military technology have made the present juncture a particularly favourable one for such a step.

We are left finally with the most serious risk: the risk of blackmail. I believe that there is no denying that total unilateral disarmament by the Western powers would leave them vulnerable to Soviet nuclear blackmail if the USSR retains its nuclear arsenal. This risk, I believe, is one which should be faced; it is a terrible risk but a risk less terrible than that of nuclear war. For our nations to be reduced to the status of Romania would be an incomparably smaller disaster than for all our cities to be reduced to the condition of Hiroshima and Nagasaki in 1945. The degree of probability of the two outcomes is not something that can be quantified in any scientific war. Whatever the Pentagon computers may simulate in their war games, what will eventually happen will depend on unpredictable human decisions on both sides.

It has been well said that the right way to reach a decision on weighing up the risks of nuclear deterrence and disarmament is to apply a version of Pascal's wager. The worst-case outcome of deterrence, nuclear devastation, is so much more catastrophic than the worst-case outcome of disarmament, Russian domination, that the course which leads to it should be avoided no matter what the relative probabilities of the two outcomes on the different strategies.

Pascal's wager is not successful as an argument for the existence of God, because it is a flight from the pursuit of truth on a matter where, on Pascal's own principles, it mattered enormously that one should obtain truth. But in adopting a policy concerning nuclear weapons we are not anxious to reach a metaphysical truth or to predict the future of the universe: we are looking for a strategy for avoiding danger under conditions of high uncertainty. Pascal's hell was a literally infinite loss; nuclear devastation cannot claim to be infinite in the same sense. But the Pascalian policy is appropriate wherever the two evils in the worst-case outcome are incommensurable in scale; and the havoc of the aftermath of nuclear war is an evil disproportionate to any political goal to be achieved by the possession of the deterrent.

Even if we attempt, then, to base our nuclear strategy on calculation of risk, I believe that disarmament – staged and cautious disarmament – is the best option. But attempts to base nuclear strategy on the calculation of risk alone leave out of account the most important moral point. This is the principle, basic to European morality since its enunciation by Socrates, that it is better to undergo wrong than to do wrong. That principle holds good even when the evils in question are, considered in isolation from the question who perpetrates them, comparable in scale. But of course the evil we would do, if we used nuclear weapons in a major war, would be incomparably greater than the evil we would suffer if the worst came to the worst after nuclear disarmament.

I turn finally to the question of the extravagance of the nuclear arms race. I shall deal with this very briefly, not because it is unimportant in itself, but because it seems to me the least of the three things wrong with our nuclear policies; and because the extravagance of the arms spending of the NATO countries is only one of many extravagances which should make us ashamed to look in the faces of the human beings whom we could help if we wished and whom we leave instead to starve and rot with disease.

Nuclear weapons are extravagant but they are not, in a sense, expensive; if you want to do a given amount of damage, they are very often incomparably the cheapest way of doing so. Moreover, a few Polaris or Poseidon submarines may alarm a potential enemy at a fraction of the cost of a conventional army large and fortified enough to scare him off. But an arms race which goes well beyond the provision of a minimum nuclear deterrent, in the pursuit of the will-o'-the-wisp of nuclear balance, is an extravagance even in terms of the Cold War. Nuclear weapons, even as things are, take up a comparatively small amount of defence spending on both sides; but the nuclear weapons over and above the minimum deterrent do not add to military capability in the way that increases in conventional forces do, and in that sense they are the most extravagant item in the military budget. The substitution of conventional weapons for, say, theatre nuclear weapons would not necessarily be cheaper in the short run. There are stages at which nuclear weapons are a cheap way of competing in the arms race. But it would be cheaper still not to compete in any such race at all, but to turn our minds to the provision of genuine defence rather than the nuclear race to the finish.

Epilogue

9

Enemies of Academic Freedom
(1984)

I feel both honoured and abashed to be speaking in this place about the enemies of academic freedom.[1] There can be few universities in the world which have devoted so much though to the definition of academic freedom and so much energy to its defence.

The enemies of academic freedom about whom I wish to speak fall into two classes: external and internal. I wish to speak of the enemies without and the enemies within. The greatest external threats to academic freedom come from ideologies and governments; and most of all from governments in the service of ideologies.

Let me explain what I mean by an ideology. An ideology is a system of ideas which is both simple enough to be grasped without special training, and ambitious enough to offer to explain essential features of human behaviour and history. It is characteristic of ideologies that they involve consequences for moral and political behaviour. Examples of ideologies in the sense defined are Marxism, Freudianism, Christianity and the various kinds of racism. As will be seen from the list, ideologies are not necessarily malign; but all of them have in common that they are not scientific. That is to say, they are either not open to empirical confirmation or falsification at all, or they are embraced with a degree of assent which goes far beyond the evidence available for their support. Because of the simplicity of their explanatory apparatus, and the powerful commitment they demand, ideologies are at the opposite pole from the rigorous and professional methods and the tentative and revisable commitment of the scientist, scholar and philosopher in the pursuit of truth.

---

[1] This lecture was delivered at the University of Cape Town, 24 July 1984.

My own first encounter with the conflict between ideology and academic freedom came under the wing of the benign ideology of Christianity, in its Roman Catholic form. As a student in a seminary in Rome, I grew accustomed to the fact that a large number of books on the library shelves bore red blobs: they were books on the index of forbidden literature, not to be read without special permission from the Holy Office. As a condition of taking any degree at the Gregorian University where I studied, one had to take an oath, the anti-modernist oath which obliged one to reject many modern theories; it went far beyond subscription to any Christian creed or church council. For my junior degrees, I took the oath with mounting qualms; when I had completed my doctoral examinations in theology, however, and been awarded my grades, I decided that I could no longer take it, and consequently was never allowed to proceed to the degree.

Of course the Catholic authorities regarded their actions as fully justified, even though there was no doubt that the banning of books and the imposition of test oaths was an infringement of academic freedom. The transmission of pure Catholic doctrine, uncontaminated by heresy, was something of incomparably greater importance that the value of academic freedom. Thus even a benign ideology is, as such, a potential enemy of academic freedom.

In more recent years I have watched friends in several countries in Eastern Europe suffer under restraints of academic freedom on a far greater scale. There the ideology imposed is a malign ideology by comparison with Christianity, and unlike Christianity it is imposed by the forces of police and government. In such countries academics lose their posts through expressing views contrary to the party line of the moment: children of dissidents are refused admission to universities because of their parents' political activities.

But there is no need for me to tell this audience of the threat presented to academic freedom by governments committed to ideologies: you have all had only too much experience of it, and your Principal, in his inaugural address, spoke movingly of the university's duty to respond, and respond vigorously, when ideology tries to inhibit scholarship.

Even in the UK we are not immune from government threat to academic freedom. For the first time, in recent months, our Department of Education and Science (DES) has intervened to attempt to alter the content of an academic course. In Britain there is an institution called the Open University. This does not mean 'a University which is open to all, regardless of race': in that sense all UK universities are open. The British Open University is one open to enrolment without strict qualifications, which teaches largely by correspondence, radio and television programmes, and printed courses. Alone among universities it is directly funded by the government; others receive public funds via a quasi-independent body of academics, the University Grants Committee. The social studies curriculum in the Open University includes a foundation course on the social context of economic activity; from time to time complaints are made that the written material of this course shows Marxist bias. The DES has now commissioned a study by a number of government economists, which found that the complaint was justified; their study was sent on by the Department to the Vice-Chancellor of the Open University with the request that he deal with the complaint. Many academics, myself included, regard this action as a threat to the most fundamental of all academic freedoms: that the content of courses should be decided by academics on academic criteria.

I understand the arguments that can be offered in justification by the DES. It is responsible for the expenditure of taxpayers' money; it must see that the money is well spent on the purposes for which it was voted and if public money is being spent on the publication of unbalanced courses, then it is being ill-spent. The DES claims to be concerned about the academic competence of the course, not its political content, and in any case it is not itself judging the course, but merely substantiating claims which it has received as complaints before handing these on to the university authorities to deal with by their own due process.

I am no Marxist, and I would not wish to see Marxist indoctrination carried out in universities, whether at public or private expense. But it seems to me a dangerous precedent for a government which is also a paymaster to take official objection to an academic course, on the grounds that it gives excessive prominence to an ideology which is opposed to the political policies of the party in power.

It may well be that the Open University will ignore the government's intervention, without penalties; it may be that on the other grounds the course queried is already due for revision. But the precedent is an alarming one, for anti-Marxists as well as for Marxists. Under a left-wing Labour minister of education I would resent an inquiry from the DES into the question whether my college's teaching contained a sufficiently substantial Marxist element.

Though I regard this development as disquieting, I realize that any problems we may have with respect to freedom to teach what we want are insignificant compared with the difficulties you have to contend with. Our freedom to research and to learn is not hampered by the banning of books, our lecturers do not have to hesitate to treat certain topics, or to express themselves candidly, for fear their class contains a police informer.

In this University you have a traditional and resounding definition of academic freedom as the right to decide 'who may teach, what may be taught, how it shall be taught, and who may be admitted to study'. This definition, splendid though it is, seems in one way remarkably broad, including some matters which be thought to relate to university autonomy rather than to academic freedom. In another way it seems excessively narrow, since it makes no mention of research and scholarship, which is surely a function of a university as integral to its role as teaching.

I have spoken so far only of threats to the freedom of what may be taught. I shall say something in a moment about threats to the freedom of who may teach and to whom. But let me first devote a little more attention to the definition of academic freedom and its essence.

Academic freedom must be distinguished on the one hand from freedom of speech, and on the other hand from academic privilege. Academic freedom overlaps with, but is not identical with, freedom of speech. Freedom of speech is a right which, in a free society, is enjoyed by all citizens and not just by academics. Academic freedom, on the other hand, is not the same as academic privilege.

In many universities academics have the right – a right not shared by members of other professions – to take sabbatical leave. I regard sabbatical leave as a valuable, and defensible, academic privilege, and I would protest against attempts to take the right away; but I could not claim that the abolition of sabbatical leave was a violation of academic freedom.

Our own problems about university admissions have concerned two things: students from overseas, and students from different kinds of school within the UK educational system.

Mrs Thatcher's first government forced universities to charge 'full-cost fees' to overseas students, above a minimum sum fixed by ministerial decision. This, at the rate of exchange then prevailing, made Oxford one of the most expensive universities in the world. We feared that students from abroad would go elsewhere, and our international character would be impaired. Most universities and colleges protested, and as a result of these protests and diplomatic representations from other countries, the situation has now partially improved.

Was the imposition of full-cost fees a violation of academic freedom? It was clearly a breach of university autonomy: universities were no longer free to fix their fees as they had once been (though this freedom had been eroded over the years). But was it against academic freedom as well? Some institutions objected to the decision on financial grounds: high fees would deter overseas students altogether, and would have the effect of reducing overall fee income. If this had been the only objection, academic freedom would not have been affected. But others objected on genuinely academic grounds: we felt, with the experience of years behind us, that for students to rub shoulders in college with members of different nationalities and races was itself a valuable part of the education we offered. So here, a violation which was essentially one of university autonomy did trench also upon academic freedom.

With regard to the admission of students within the UK our problem in Oxford has been to ensure that our intake is fair to those from both the state and the private sector of education. Though the independent, fee-charging schools educate only a very small percentage of the population, they produce something like half the successful candidates for Oxford entry. Naturally many question whether this is fair; and we have recently revised our admissions procedures, particularly with respect to the timing of the entrance examination, in ways which we believe will make the competition for entry more visibly fair. But we have refused to accept the suggestion (made this time by the opposition party, not by the government) that we should fix quotas of entry for different kinds of school. Some of our own number would favour such a move: but that would be, in my view, an improper use of non-academic criteria in the academic decision on admission to the university.

Academic freedom is the freedom conferred on academics to enable them to carry out well the academic tasks of the university, the pursuit of unknown truth by research and scholarship, and the passing on of acquired learning by publication and teaching. So academic freedom is freedom from constraint in the performance of these academic activities.

Among the most important of the decisions made by the university in aid of the pursuit and tradition of truth is the choice of the persons to hold academic posts, and this is a choice which must be made on academic grounds. Limitation of the choice on other grounds is a violation of academic freedom.

In many parts of the world, especially those like the UK where unemployment is high, this aspect of academic freedom is under threat. In the UK any foreigner who wishes to work must obtain a work permit; and for an employer to obtain a work permit he must show not just that the prospective employee is the best qualified person for the job, but that he is the only person qualified.

My own college recently experienced the constraints which this system imposes when we advertized a junior research fellowship in history. In open competition among candidates working in various fields, the preferred candidate was an expert in medieval siege warfare. When we elected him and applied for a work permit, we were refused permission unless we could certify that he was the only fit candidate. This we were unwilling to do: had he declined the post we would have elected the next best applicant. Nor were we willing to leave the post unfilled and advertise for an expert on the medieval mangonel – a post for which he would undoubtedly have been the only candidate. We wanted to preserve the right, which we regarded as precious, of appointing persons academically best qualified for posts, irrespective of nationality. After months of negotiations eventually a formula was hit upon which seemed to satisfy both parties. Nowadays when we apply for a work permit for a foreign academic we testify 'A.B. was so far ahead of the other candidates in the competition as to be, in effect, uniquely qualified for the post advertized.'

The freedom to be able to choose whom to teach is much the most controversial of the freedoms contained in your definition of academic freedom. It is rightly included in the definition, I would contend, only in so far as this freedom of choice serves the academic function of the university. What is essential is the freedom to admit to a university on academic criteria, rather than on irrelevant grounds such as racial origin. In the UK we are forbidden to base our admissions on racial grounds; and I do not regard this as an infringement of academic freedom.

I do not claim that it is necessary that those most successful in competitive examination on entry should be admitted in preference to those less successful. Whether this is – even on strictly academic grounds – the best way of choosing the candidates, depends on the whole context of education within which a university operates. It is perfectly rational to choose a candidate who has done poorly in an examination if, having discounted any disadvantage which he may have suffered in preparation, we believe that he is likely to profit from a university education as well as one who has performed better on the basis of schooling better adapted for examination coaching. To choose in this way on the basis of promise rather than performance is something quite different from imposing a quota of entrants from various sources; it is academically perfectly justified, even though naturally it involves risks of misjudgement greater than those involved in basing admissions on unqualified competitive examination.

The imposition of quotas, on the other hand, whether on grounds of race, or sex, or religion, or background, seems to me a violation of academic freedom. It is often imposed for excellent motives, out of a desire to assist disadvantaged groups. But no student in a university should have to believe 'I am here in this university only because I am a black, or a woman, or because I come from a state school.'

The threat to academic freedom in the imposition of quotas is no less real if it is imposed from within the university: for there are enemies of academic freedom within as well as without the academy. The enemies within fall into two classes: enemies within the faculty, and enemies within the students.

Faculty members most commonly threaten academic freedom by abusing it. One does a disservice to academic freedom if one uses one's academic position to impose an ideology on one's students, if one awards grades on inappropriate criteria, if one harasses one's students sexually. In particular it is a disaster for academic freedom if academics try to turn every issue of academic privilege into an issue of academic freedom. This abuse is compounded when academic privilege is defended by means which are a contradiction of its *raison d'etre*; as when the comparative wage-scales of academics are defended by the campus equivalent of industrial action. When academics seek to promote their own interests by acts or omissions whose immediate effect is to damage their own students, they disgrace their privileged profession. It is true that all strikes tend to injure innocent third parties, as a dockers' strike may inconvenience holidaymakers, but there is something offensive about a strike that causes injury to those to whom one is professionally placed in a pastoral relationship.

Academics can sin against academic freedom not only by smuggling in, under that name, less noble privileges; they can also err by overvaluing even genuine academic freedom. Academic freedom is a genuine value, and a precious one; but it does not come very high in the hierarchy of human values. The right to academic freedom is not as important as the right to a living wage, or the right to live where one chooses, or the right not to be forcibly separated from one's family. A society which sets a high value on academic freedom and a low value on the other rights may be, *sub specie aeternitatis*, far worse than a society which denies academic freedom while respecting the more elemental human rights.

The second class of enemies of academic freedom which are enemies within are the enemies drawn from the student body of the university. In recent decades, in many countries, some of the worst attacks on academic freedom have come from the students who are the primary beneficiaries of the academy. The interruption of lectures and seminars, the persecution of unpopular teachers and administrators, the use of force and threat as a way of determining academic decisions – all these are violations of academic freedom which both interfere with due academic process itself, and bring not only academic freedom, but the whole academic community itself, into disrepute. They thus give pretexts to malevolent public authorities to interfere in academic life, and fuel hostility to academic values among the philistine public.

In saying this I am not denying or wishing to abridge the right of students to protest, and by demonstrating to exhibit their opposition to political policies of governments, or non-academic decisions of academic bodies. If students boycott a college hall to protest cafeteria prices, or mount a noisy lobby of a committee to fix room rents, however annoying this may be to university administrators, this cannot be said to be any diminution of academic freedom. It is a diffrent matter when direct action is used to bring pressure to bear on academic appointments, or the content of lecture courses, or the results of examinations.

The clearest violations of academic freedom by students occur when physical action is taken to prevent a lecturer from giving a lecture, or to prevent a student from attending a course. Both kinds of violation are, alas, still not unknown in my own country. I think then one of the prime demands of academic freedom is that every lecturer duly appointed, and every student duly enrolled, should be free to give or take their courses.

This seems to be beyond dispute where what is at issue is academics giving courses, and students attending courses, within their own university run by the university's own faculty. The matter becomes more difficult when we consider lectures and speeches within a university given by visitors from outside.

So far as concerns academic visitors – staff or students of other universities – invited by members of the university, it seems to me that the rule should be the same as with courses organized within the university. The common franchise of the community of scholars should mean that any member of one university, appropriately invited by members of another, should have the same right to be heard as faculty and students of the inviting university; and should, moreover, have that right enforced, if necessary, by the university authorities.

We move into a more difficult area when we consider non-academic visitors. Must every member of academic staff have the right to invite anyone he or she wishes to address his or her course? And must that right be enforced by the university authorities at whatever cost this may entail?

I note that the Senate and Council of the University of Cape Town recently affirmed support for freedom of speech and associ-ation on the campus, and asserted the right of academics to invite any person to take part in any academic programme. I must confess to some misgivings about the apparent breadth of this declaration. I realize that it was accompanied with a reaffirmation of the right to dissent against such invitations, or views expressed provided that the expression of such dissent in no way limited freedom of expression or speech. But if it means that it is an essential part of academic freedom that *any* academic can invite anyone to speak officially on campus, then I beg to differ.

Some invitations issued by academics can themselves amount to an abuse of academic freedom: thus there can be invitations to those who expound views so evil, or represent regimes so ob-noxious, that they amount to such an abuse. I think that there is no violation of academic freedom if the academic body as a whole – through its appropriate governing body – is given the oversight of invitations to non-academic persons. An invitation to a practising, non-academic politician, for example, may well be something that needs to be approved by a senate before being issued.

I agree, then, with the proposition that academics should be free to invite whom they will, but not any individual academic. If an invitation is likely to involve the need for university policing, or disciplinary action in its enforcement, then, in the case of an invitation to an academic, the academic authorities should be notified; if a non-academic is involved, then the academic authori-ties should give their consent.

I realize that in expressing this opinion I am touching on a matter which has been a subject of concern here in recent times;

but the rule which I have enunciated was formulated on the basis of a partly parallel experience in Oxford.

To apply the rule to a fictitious case: if a colleague of mine invited an academic from a South African university to report on the operation of the race laws, I would regard that as a legitimate use of his academic freedom, and extend the College's protection to the lecturer, even if there were violent demonstrations by students. But if he invited the South African Ambassador I would regard that as an abuse of academic freedom. Since the invitation involved a non-academic visitor, I would regard it as one which required the approval of the appropriate governing body and in the governing body I would endeavour to have the visit forbidden on two grounds; first, that any academic purpose to be served by such a visit could be served by other means; and secondly that an ambassador is not an academic but a representative of a government; so that offering a platform is a measure of support of that government's policies.

I have said that if a South African academic was invited to visit my college I would regard this as an academic right to be defended, and indeed we have been honoured and delighted over a number of years to welcome distinguished scholars from South Africa, and from the University of Cape Town in particular, who have adorned our common rooms and enlivened our seminars. From this you will have concluded that I do not favour an academic boycott of South Africa.

You will know that there are those of my academic colleagues in the UK who will think I should not have come to this country and indeed that the Association of University Teachers has as its official policy a boycott of South African universities.

Before I close, therefore, I must say a few words about boycotts, academic and otherwise.

There are, I suppose, six main kinds of boycott being practised, or promoted, against South Africa by nationals of other countries: a consumer boycott of SA exports; a boycott on sporting links; a boycott on theatrical and entertainment links; ecclesiastical excommunications; a refusal to invest in South Africa; and a severance of academic contact. The arguments used for each of these boycotts vary somewhat from case to case, but all of them are justified on the grounds that only by bringing home to decision-makers in this country the isolation of South Africa in the world community can pressure be brought to bear on the government to repeal unjust laws and abandon racist policies.

I shall mention only briefly the first four boycotts. Like most English liberals, I have practised for years, in general, a boycott of South African imports; but I am aware that the arguments on this topic are fairly finely balanced (Who gets hurt most by such a boycott? What would those who are most hurt by it, in South Africa, want us to do?) and aware also that any effect of my action is in any case insignificant. With regard to the sporting and entertainments bans, while being in principle in favour, I realize that these are issues on which I have not had to take any personal decisions, and therefore ones to which I have not had to devote detailed thought. Similarly with regard to the ecclesiastical proceedings of excommunication of South African churches. It is not so with the economic and academic boycotts: both of these are matters to which I have had to give attention both in connection with personal and institutional decisions.

Most Oxford colleges have substantial private endowments and derive a proportion of their annual income from dividends rather than from fees. They are likely to hold part of their funds in international equity portfolio, and therefore they have to consider the question whether they should invest in South Africa. My own college's policy has been for many years that it does not invest in any South African company, and has given instruction to our brokers to that effect.

Many companies based in London or elsewhere do, of course, operate in South Africa; and in Oxford there have been many arguments about the correct investment policy in this case. On the one side, it is argued that whatever arguments there are against direct investment in South Africa are equally strong against indirect investment; on the other hand, it is argued that if one did not invest in any London company which had any South African operation there would be so few 'clean' companies left that one would not be able to fulfil one's duty, as a trustee, to obtain a reasonable return on investment. 'Disinvestment' anyway, it is argued, is likely to be totally ineffective as a way of bringing any pressure to bear on companies, who will be only too pleased to be rid of troublesome shareholders.

This dilemma is resolved by a number of investing institutions including my own, by continuing to hold shares in the companies in question, but by being active shareholders and monitoring the companies' activities in South Africa to see that they accord with various ethical standards such as the EEC code of conduct or the Sullivan principles.

In this qualified sense, therefore, the institution to which I belong operates an economic boycott of South Africa. How can this be reconciled with the opposition of myself and my colleagues to the academic boycott?

There is, I believe, no inconsistency here. It is clear at the outset that visiting a country in itself in no way implies support for the government or the government's policies. By coming to South Africa academics are no more expressing support of apartheid than by going to Czechoslovakia they are supporting the oppressive regime there. This point can, of course, be made in connection with all boycotts; but there are, I believe, three ways in which academic links differ from sporting, cultural and economic ones.

First, because of the nature of the republic of letters. There is, no doubt, an international community of sportsmen as there is an international community of scholars and scientists. But the international character is not as intrinsic to sport as it is to science and learning. It is more essential to the scholarly enterprise that scholars should share a give and take of ideas with their colleagues in other countries than it is to skaters or tennis players that they should compete against players from other countries. Just as we believe that no one should be excluded from access to the republic of letters because of their race or creed, so we believe that no one should be excluded from free circulation within the republic of letters because of the regime they live under.

Secondly, it is much easier, in the case of an academic, to separate out from the academic purpose of the visit any appearance of support for apartheid. A spokesman for Equity, announcing his intention of terminting the boycott, is reported to have said 'I abhor apartheid as much as ever, but it is better to denounce it in South Africa than in London.' If he intends, when he gets to South

Africa to denounce apartheid, I wish him well, but it is not easy for an actor in the course of his acting to do so. But for an academic – certainly for a philosopher or social scientist – it will commonly be natural for him, in the course of his normal activity of lecturing, and conducting seminars, to make plain where he stands.

It remains to mention the third and most important reason for opposing a boycott of universities such as the University of Cape Town. Those who are affected by such a boycott are not the South African government or the supporters of its policy, but rather those who have fought those policies bravely and provided a focus of opposition for them in difficult times – namely, yourselves who have devoted yourselves to the idea of a university whose character is determined by scholarship and not by ethnicity.

As my lecture has illustrated, we too have problems in defending academic freedom; but they are as nothing compared with the threats against which you have had to battle. The threats which governments make to our academic freedom are mild by comparison with those made to you, and when we speak out against government encroachments we need not fear that our protests are being filed in a dossier or that our passports will be removed.

Any visitor to your university must congratulate you on the battle you have fought in recent years to open access to the university to all races, and look forward to the day of your complete victory.

Index